NAIL
THE
JOB

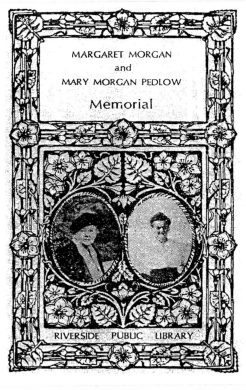

NAIL THE JOB

Every Tool You'll Need to Land Your Dream Job

THE EDITORS OF
MBA JUNGLE AND
JD JUNGLE MAGAZINES

PERSEUS
PUBLISHING

A Member of the Perseus Books Group

Copyright © 2002 by Jungle Media Group

Library of Congress Control Number: 2002112433
ISBN 0–7382–0744–6

Perseus Publishing is a Member of the Perseus Books Group.
Find us on the World Wide Web at http://www.perseuspublishing.com.

Perseus Publishing books are available at special discounts for bulk purchases in the U.S. by corporations, institutions, and other organizations. For more information, please contact the Special Markets Department at the Perseus Books Group, 11 Cambridge Center, Cambridge, MA 02142, or call (800) 255-1514 or (617) 252-5298, or e-mail j.mccrary@perseusbooks.com.

Text design by Brent Wilcox
Set in 11.5-point Minion by the Perseus Books Group

First printing, December 2002
1 2 3 4 5 6 7 8 9 10—06 05 04 03 02

CONTENTS

Contents

JUNGLE CONTRIBUTORS

Portions of this book have appeared previously in *MBA Jungle* and *JD Jungle* magazines, as well as in mbajungle.com. Many of the articles have been updated and expanded for this book. A special thanks to these and other contributors below.

"Cover Letters That Cook," by Hal Levey

"The Art of the Resumé," by Hal Levey and Sara Goldsmith

"The Perfect Thank-You Note," by Lisa Chudnofsky

"Moving Stationery," by Lisa Chudnofsky

"What to Say After the Beep," by Paul Scott and Hal Levey

"Laying the Network," by Mickey Butts and Alexis Offen

"How to Work a Room," by Jeff Ousborne

"The Ultimate Recruiting Playbook," by David Blend and Jacob Kalish

"Networking on Uncle Sam's Dime," by John Bishop

"Dining for Dollars," by Paul Scott

"Get on Board," by Christopher Rapp

"The Anatomy of an Interview," "Size Up Your Interviewer in Sixty Seconds," and "Every Second Counts," by David Blend, Lisa Chudnofsky, and Maria Spinella

Contributors

"Body Language: It's Not What You Said," by David Blend

"Nail the Recruiting Dinner," by Paul Scott

"Interviewing at a Consulting Firm," by Michael K. Norris

"Interviewing on Wall Street," by Jeff Ousborne

"Interviewing at a Law Firm," by Dimitra Kessenides

"Interviewing at a Start-Up," by Laurina Gibbs

"Moving into Banking," "Moving into Consulting," and "Moving into Marketing," by Paul Scott

"Banking on the Wrong Headhunters" and "Tips for Happy Hunting," by Hal Levey and David Blend

"Dissect the Job Offer," by Paul Scott and Karen Auerbach

"The Give-and-Take," by Paul Scott and Paul Marchand

CHAPTER 1

Introduction: Nail the Job

YOU'VE GOT A FIRM HANDSHAKE, RIGHT? OWN AT least one nice, conservative suit. Comb your hair on at least a fortnightly basis. Bet you're smart, too. Went to a good school. Maybe you've even got a graduate degree. And some experience, listed on a resumé that's crisp, clean, and sprinkled with enough action verbs to fill three *Lethal Weapon* scripts. And of course, you're personable. Charming, even. Not to mention hardworking, dedicated, ambitious, respectful, and eager. A great team player. Just the kind of person we're looking for here at XYZ Enterprises. Fan-freaking-tastic. Now get in the back of the line, pal.

Good enough isn't good enough anymore. Actually, good enough has never been good enough. Not to land the job you really want. The one you dream about. The one you know, deep down, you *deserve*. It's a simple matter of supply and demand. As long as the supply of challenging, reward-

ing, high-paying jobs is low—and it almost always is, regardless of the state of the economy—the demand for them
from other qualified job-seekers means you're facing more
competition than a Japanese Buick dealer. Or look at it this
way: As long as there's a seemingly inexhaustible supply of
eager young resumé-peddlers storming America's corporate
Bastille, desirable employers are going to demand that you
offer them a heck of a lot more than "good enough."

There is no margin for error. You've got to *nail* it. Nail the
search. Nail the networking. Nail the interview. Nail the job.
And that's where this book comes in. It offers advice from
industry insiders and top-notch experts to help you close
the gap that separates the very good candidate from the one
who gets the job. It's a book for anyone who's ever asked,
"What's *she* got that I haven't got?" or "What makes *him* so
great?" It's a book full of original, thoughtful, and often
clever tips that spell the difference between "We'll be in
touch" and "When can you start?"

This is not *Job Search for Dummies*. We have no use for
dummies—except perhaps when we're crash-testing a fresh
shipment of conference-room chairs. If you're looking for
information on how to read the classifieds, you're holding
the wrong book. Want to know how to make it in Hollywood? We'd recommend one of the other fine volumes
you'll find three aisles down. Much of this book's content
originally appeared in *MBA Jungle* magazine, which means
it concerns itself largely with the most sought-after business
jobs: finance, consulting, and marketing. But it's not only

for MBAs, to be sure. Most of the advice and strategies presented here would benefit anyone seeking a job at any level in any highly competitive business field. Including, most likely, you.

So let's get started. We assume you're smart. We assume you're presentable. We assume you're qualified. And we assume you'll thank us in a noisy, public fashion when you're rich and famous. Just kidding.

CHAPTER 2

The Perfect Pitch

HERE'S A SAFE BET: THE NUMBER OF HANDWRITTEN thank-you notes you've sent to prospective employers equals the number of Neil Diamond records in your collection. Which is to say, nada. Zero. Zilch. If this is true for you, you should change your tune. Thank-you notes, like perfectly crafted resumés and well-timed follow-up phone calls, are not meaningless formalities to be quickly dispensed with now that e-mail has made communication so breezy ("Hey, love what you guys are doing. Resumé attached. Call me on my cell."). And thank-you notes to the interviewer are just one of many pieces of peripheral correspondence that should become second nature. Sure, you can download a fancy resumé template in a matter of seconds these days, but it's still just as important to sweat over the quality of your writing and the content of your message. How well you communicate before and after an interview is almost as important as what you say once you're actually in the hot seat. Think of it this way—if your cover letter is a clunker, an employer might fear you would be just as graceless when introducing yourself to clients. Here, a bevy of tips to make sure the first impressions you leave are, in fact, impressive.

Cover Letters That Cook

Cover letters may seem an anachronism, like three-martini lunches and Internet millionaires. Yet these pithy introductions play a key role in job hunting. For a recruiter, a cover letter can be a small window into what makes you tick and, if you get it right, a reason for a company to take your resumé seriously. Here's an example of a cover letter that's spot-on, complete with footnotes to help you compose one of your own.

June 23, 2003

Ms. Elaine Curacold
Incomplete Investments, Inc.
123 Mayfield Lane
New York, NY 10000

Dear Ms. Curacold,[1]

I'm very interested in the job opening at Incomplete Investments, Inc., for an associate portfolio manager. Incomplete Investments Vice President Reed Bachman, who was my manager when we both worked at ClearCut Bank, suggested I contact you about the position.[2]

My four years of experience as an analyst with ClearCut Bank have fully prepared me to handle the duties you require of an associate portfolio manager.[3] At ClearCut, I researched companies in a number of industries, including information technology and telecommunications—sectors favored by Incomplete Investments. My managers gave me high marks for being able to quickly deconstruct balance sheets and cash flow statements while keeping an eye on big picture trends.[4]

In early 2002, I voluntarily left ClearCut to work for a United Nations relief agency in Mexico. My fluency in Spanish could be an asset to your firm's emerging-markets research.[5]

I'll call you at 11 A.M. on Thursday, July 3, in hopes that we can discuss the position.[6] In the meantime, if you need any additional information, please do not hesitate to contact me at home (212-555-1234) or on my cell phone (917-865-2229).[7, 8]

Sincerely,

Len A. Little
12345 6th Street
New York, NY 10000
len@net-buzz.com[9]

Enclosures[10]

The Footnotes

(1) **Keep It Formal.**   Whether you're sending your cover letter via regular mail or e-mail, don't succumb to the informality of the Internet. "If you send a cover letter by e-mail that starts with 'Hi,' it and your resumé will probably end up in the trash," says Cynthia Shore, former assistant dean at the University of Buffalo's School of Management and director of its career resource center. Treat an e-mail as you would a proper letter: Instead of "Hi," open with "Dear Mr. Case." Instead of "Thanks," conclude with "Sincerely."

(2) Drop Names Carefully.   Sure, mentioning the name of someone you know at the company you're targeting might get you a second glance from HR folks, but be careful with how you present the relationship. Name-droppers walk a fine line, says Jana Carlson, a professional recruiter at the investment firm Blackstone Group, and could cross that line if they play up a relationship that doesn't really exist. "We're a large company, but we're not so big that I can't send an e-mail to the reference asking how well they know an applicant," says Carlson. If you've puffed up your connections, you'll likely be tossed aside. But accurately revealing certain commonalities—perhaps several execs at the company graduated from your alma mater—shows that you have done your homework and targeted your search well.

(3) Do You Relate?   Think of the letter as a summation of who you are and why you're applying. "You can use the cover letter as a marketing tool, and you can relate your skills to the fit of a given organization," says Allyn Curry, associate director of corporate relations at Indiana University's Kelley School of Business.

(4) Be Coy About Money.   Don't include a salary requirement, even when the job description requests it. You don't want to price yourself out of a job or undervalue your skills.

(5) Fill In the Gaps.   Use the cover letter to briefly explain hiccups or unusual gaps in your work experience rather than to cleverly hide them. If you were involved in a failed company, put a positive spin on the experience: Perhaps you learned how to manage up or the right way to perform due diligence on an acquisition. If you took time off to see the world or be with your family, that's "perfectly acceptable, within reason," says Susan Levine, manager of marketing recruiting at Bain & Company. Adds Laurie Boockvar, associate director at Columbia Business School's Office of MBA Career Services: "Not everyone has been able to have a linear career path and move steadily without life interrupting."

(6) Follow Up—For Sure.   There's nothing wrong with sending out your cover letter and resumé, sitting back, and waiting for an interview invite—unless, of course, you want a job. Elizabeth O. Sullivan, a lecturer and communications specialist for the Jesse H. Jones Graduate School of Management at Rice University, recommends stating in a cover letter exactly when you will follow up with a phone call. And make sure to do so. The call will help keep your name in the forefront of a recruiter's memory, and it will separate you from more timid souls. If you get the contact person's voice mail, leave a polite message saying you'll call back at a later time. But never use a cell phone. "People assume they are being heard, but sometimes they're not," says Laura S. Bassin, associate director of career services at the Fordham Graduate School of Business Administration. Cellular transmissions can break up before you leave your contact information ("You can reach me at 617-555-12—") and you won't even know it.

(7) Tell 'Em How to Reach You.   One of the worst ways to fumble a job opportunity is to miss the invitation to interview. Roommates can erase phone messages. E-mails can be inadvertently deleted or lost in cyberspace. Therefore, your cover letter should indicate the best way a potential employer can reach you. According to Cindy Neale, a spokesperson with AT&T, "Corporate recruiters like to exercise discretion, so let them know if you'd prefer e-mail, cell phone, or any other number in addition to your home phone."

(8) Keep It Short.   Brevity is the soul of wit, Shakespeare wrote, and it's also the hallmark of a good cover letter. "Your letter is probably going to get a thirty-second scan from the employer," says Curry. So keep it as succinct as possible: four paragraphs, tops, and never more than a single page.

(9) Tech Check.   When e-mailing materials, make sure attachments can be downloaded and opened without difficulty. Send them to a friend and have him check that the attachments open and look fine, says Bassin. Garbled or incomplete documents will get a quick trip into an employer's virtual trash bin.

(10) Candy Is for Kids.   The medium counts less than the message, so steer clear of eye-popping graphics, exotic fonts, or brightly colored paper. Curry recalls an incident in which a graduating MBA sent a very creative cover letter and resumé on colored paper to an advertising business. He got some attention all right: The company hung his handiwork on a bulletin board and the student became a laughingstock. The lesson, Curry says, is that "the key to being effective is all in the use of words."

The Art of the Resumé

Crafting a resumé can be like sculpting a statue. You start with a rough block of text. Then you begin to steadily chip away at it, shaping and polishing your words again and again until the resumé emerges, a perfect, elegant thing of beauty. All it takes is one false move—maybe a font that's too small or including your date of birth—and your resumé could be tossed aside. Here's how to make it museum quality.

Everything in Order, Sir?   Avoid organizing your work experience according to your previous titles, types of employers, or some other category. These unusual approaches will make recruiters wonder what you're trying to hide. Use the traditional chronological format, starting with your most recent gig, even if you spent a wayward year as a lion tamer.

You're Not Grocery Shopping.   Most people fall into the trap of just listing job responsibilities like groceries on a scrap of paper: "Managed marketing group," or "Analyzed cost reports." To get your resumé noticed, use cause and effect to highlight your accomplishments and showcase results (i.e., "Implemented cost-cutting in 500-person engineering department, lowering expenses by 20 percent with no decline in productivity").

A Well-Tailored Resumé.   If you are angling for a job as an investment analyst covering health care, why play up your experience with database software companies? Emphasize the experience and education that best fits the requirements of the job you're targeting. Which means you should have a slightly different resumé prepared for each type of job you seek.

Well-Rounded, Too.   Even if all of your past jobs involved shredding documents, highlight the responsibilities that were different for each gig rather than repeating the same thing over and over again. This way, you'll look like a well-rounded shredder, and companies do like to hire the well-rounded sorts.

The One-Page Rule.   Most recruiters recommend limiting your resumé to one page. But if you have extensive experience in the field you're targeting, you can stretch this rule a bit, as long as the additional information is vital and not found elsewhere on your resumé. Nothing is worse than a CV that's both long and repetitive.

Numbers Must Add Up. When quantifying your accomplishments with numbers, use discretion. Brandishing borderline performance numbers signals a lack of experience and bad judgment. "Phrases like 'Managed a budget of $500,000' or 'Led a team of two' might catch my eye in a bad way," says Olaf Weckesser, a former recruiter for McKinsey & Company. Better to spin it as "Managed company's largest budget." Adds Alexandra DeMarino, a Citigroup recruiter: "If a small number is impressive, you absolutely have to put it in context."

Off-Key Words. Some companies—fewer than 25 percent—use scanners to locate certain keywords in resumés. So making your resumé scanner-friendly might help your chances. Use plain white paper, put your name at the top of the page, make sure to put line breaks between sections, and sparingly use appropriate keywords the company includes in the job description. But resumés appear contrived when candidates overuse such terms. Describing a business-development position using such terms as *needs assessment* and *contract analysis* in order to squeeze in more keywords could hurt you more than help you.

Don't Get Too Personal. "If you mention your age, we have to trash your resumé," says Jeremy Eskenazi, former vice president of talent acquisition at Idealab!, the California incubator firm. Since it's illegal for a company to solicit a candidate's age, race, or marital status during the hiring process, firms have adopted a "don't tell" policy to avoid potential bias suits. Many won't risk even having it handed to them.

Play It Both Ways.   Strike a balance between showing personal initiative ("Led the marketing department's reorganization") and demonstrating teamwork ("Collaborated in product design"). Both are essential, so don't downplay your accomplishments or neglect to acknowledge team successes.

Wise Fonts.   Another reason not to use fancy fonts: They can turn to gibberish if sent by e-mail. Helvetica or Times New Roman fonts are easy to read on paper and in e-mail. Also keep in mind that after plowing through resumés all day, the last thing a recruiter wants to do is squint in order to make out your name. Best to use at least 11- or 12-point type.

Fancy Doesn't Help.   And while we're at it, eliminate all bells and whistles. "A recruiter who receives resumés in pretty plastic folders will likely toss them," says Dave Opton, former VP of personnel for Sterling Drug International. "I just don't have time to take the damn things apart." Another faux pas: Folding a resumé so that it fits into a standard business envelope. Heavy-stock paper that retains its crease can be a nuisance. As Opton points out, "They're easier to store and photocopy if they're flat." Also, don't try to differentiate your resumé with boxes, bars, or ornate lettering. When recruiters see a resumé that's designed differently, they think the person is trying to create a diversion. Instead, focus on content and your resumé will rise to the top of the pile.

Proofreed. Rereading your CV a few times—and then having a friend or colleague look it over—before sending it out may be one of the most important steps in the job process. We've all heard horror stories about the words computer spell-checkers miss, to the eternal embarrassment of the job-seeker: "pubic" instead of "public," "reed" instead of "read." But you should also keep an eye out for accuracy in the dates on your resumé. One MBA career services official recalls the time a student went into an interview with a resumé listing 1898 as the start date for a position—and being asked by the recruiter if she was a vampire.

Electronically Speaking. To send your resumé via e-mail, remove all formatting, including bullet points (use dashes or asterisks instead). Then both paste it into an e-mail *and* attach the document so that the recruiter can use whichever is easier. Some people won't open an attachment for fear of a virus, and others are simply too busy to want to fuss with it.

The Perfect Thank-You Note

Ask human resource managers about thank-you notes these days and you'll hear stories of a lost art. "A few years ago, if a candidate didn't send a handwritten thank-you note, I remembered it; now, it's the opposite," says Michelle McCallion, a former recruiter for PricewaterhouseCoopers. A quick e-mail is okay. A two-line note is better. But to really blow the doors off the barn, sit down with a crisp sheet of stationery and thank 'em like no one else will.

Perfect Timing

For starters, drop an e-mail after the meeting. How fast should you be on the trigger? "It's by no means a sign of overeagerness to send a note immediately after the interview," says Jill Borteck, a former recruiter for Merrill Lynch. "I'd take notice if I met someone at 3:00, they left at 4:00, and I had an e-mail in my in box by 4:30. That would make me think, 'Wow, this person is on the ball.'" Sean Huurman, director of recruiting at KPMG Consulting, agrees: "The interview game is not like the dating game. This is no time to be coy. We're looking for people with initiative and drive, and you need to show us you have those qualities."

Follow up the e-mail by dropping a bona fide paper letter in the mailbox the morning after the interview, suggests Lydia Ramsey, a business etiquette expert and the author of *Manners That Sell*. The effort it takes to address an envelope reflects your eagerness to be a part of the firm. Many recruiters say that they prefer pen to printer: "I'll remember a handwritten note even more, because it's different," says McCallion. Unless, of course, "different" for you means "illegible." In that case, type it. Either way, make sure your name and phone number are easy to spot.

Short and Sweet

"The entire note shouldn't take more than a minute to read," says Borteck. That means about 150 words. Reiterate your skills succinctly, and relate them to the company's specific objectives. If the interviewer mentioned that the company is targeting growth in Asia, remind her that your experience—say, marketing a Japan-based product—would help boost growth.

Never slip into biz speak. Generic buzzwords like *self-starter* and *strong leader* make you seem . . . generic. The best way to communicate your leadership on paper is to avoid starting every sentence with the word "I"—twice is more than enough. By mixing it up, you'll subtly set yourself apart from all the other "I" hounds.

Another trick: Quote something the interviewer said ("The 'bottom-to-top management philosophy' you mentioned is intriguing"), and then extrapolate on it ("A verbal evaluation process might be a good addition to the written one"). "People love to have their own words repeated back to them," says Ramsey. "It tells them that you were really paying attention." And, of course, it flatters the hell out of them.

Target Audience

You never know who's going to have a say in whether you get hired, so collect a business card from each person you meet, and send a note to everyone who took the time to talk with you about the company. Personalizing each one multiplies a note's effectiveness. And should it circulate, your note won't look like an uncreative form letter.

Proofread

No matter how many times you've read a note, have someone else look at it. "Errors in a note can certainly make a difference and raise a question about your fitness for a job," says KPMG's Huurman. Not dotting your i's and crossing your t's—literally—could cost you a job you're being considered for.

Signing Off

"I look forward to speaking with you again," followed by "Sincerely," is perfect.

Moving Stationery

You're pumping out cover letters, resumés, and thank-you notes like a wartime bullet factory. Your prose couldn't be more eloquent if it were in iambic pentameter. Why waste your words on low-grade paper? We asked topflight stationers for inside information on choosing and designing the perfect personal stationery. Because when you're not sitting in the recruiter's office with shined shoes and smart answers, the piece of paper with your name on top had better be a darn good substitute.

Shopping Around

When buying stationery, ask for help as soon as you walk into a store. At top-notch shops, new staff must study *Crane's Blue Book of Stationery*, a trove of product-related tips. (Example: Upon meeting a business contact at a social event, don't exchange business cards; instead, hand over a 3½-by-2-inch "social business card," printed with name and number only.) If you're job hunting, bring letterhead samples from companies where you'd like to work. This will help a salesperson suggest styles in keeping with the companies' vibe.

Finer Qualities

Brightly colored paper is bush league. Stick with plain white or ecru (also called natural or ivory), says Melanie Nerenberg, director of marketing for Kate's Paperie in Manhattan and Connecticut. When it comes to finish, a good choice is wove, which is smooth (there's also laid, which has a rich, textured pattern). A paper's weight classification is determined by weighing 2,000 regular 8½-by-11-inch sheets of it. Increments start at nine pounds and go through the thirties. The higher the better—more heft reduces flimsiness and increases opaqueness, so the type won't bleed through the back. The recommended weight for business stationery is 24, but a few high-end brands offer a 32-pounder. Anything below 20? Toilet paper.

What's Inside

A paper's weight isn't as important as its cotton-fiber content, or rag. A 20-pound sheet of 100 percent rag is of finer quality than a 24-pounder that's only 25 percent rag. As Sean Bradley, manager of Soolip Paperie & Press in West Hollywood, says, "Some paper can be really thick and heavy, but it's still floppy." Cotton gives paper a crisp feeling not unlike new cash. Among the top manufacturers of 100 percent rag paper are Southworth, William Arthur, and Crane's, the company that makes the paper used for U.S. currency.

Pure and Simple

When printing your name on stationery, steer clear of fancy fonts. Opt for the clarity of Times New Roman or Copperplate. Simplicity also applies to ink color. Black is fine, but midnight blue or charcoal lends a subtle, something's-different-here quality to set the stationery apart. Text should appear on the side where the watermark, or manufacturer's logo, reads correctly. There are four options for printing: flat, for a matte finish; thermography, for a slightly raised, glossy look; engraving, for a three-dimensional print with sharp lines; and letterpress, for an indented matte finish. Which style you choose is a matter of taste, but for business correspondence, Oriana Vanderlind, an assistant buyer at the Fairfield, California-based stationer Papyrus, rates thermography first, flat second, engraving third, and letterpress last (flat printing and thermography are the least expensive). At Kate's Paperie, a set of fifty engraved social sheets or cards with fifty engraved envelopes runs about $300.

Return to Sender

Never use return-address labels—stickers will undermine your effort to create a sophisticated look. Print your return address on the top left of business envelopes and on the back flap of social-sheet envelopes. A classy finishing touch: Line the envelopes with the same color ink as the engraving. But that's it for frills. Though you've invested hours of time and care in the stationery, it should appear effortlessly professional—just like everything else about your presentation.

What to Say After the Beep

Voice-mail messages play a pivotal supporting role in the job search, giving a boost to your resumé and interview. Your message better be a good one, because it's competing against some 375 communiqués—including e-mails, phone calls, faxes, and letters—that the average executive receives daily, according to a study conducted by Pitney Bowes, a messaging solutions company. In this environment, any excuse that a job-seeker gives an exec to delete a voice mail before listening to it—even five slightly rambling seconds—is a valid one.

Be Strategic.   Just because it's easy to leave a voice message doesn't mean you should do so every day, unless you want the word *pest* scrawled across your resumé. Leave a message a week or so after you've sent a resumé to a company, unless, of course, you've been requested not to do so. A voice message after you've interviewed with the firm and sent a thank-you letter can be even more effective in making sure you're not forgotten.

Getting Started.   The single worst thing to do is to clutter the beginning of a message with useless information (phone-tag jokes most certainly qualify). According to Jacqueline Whitmore, founder of the Protocol School of Palm Beach, Florida, the superfluous pleasantries so many people rely on to start their messages make a distinctly negative impression on busy executives. "Don't say, 'I hope you're having a good day,'" she explains. "That's a cliché that doesn't mean anything." Instead, signal that you won't waste the person's time—state your name and that you're following up on your resumé or interview. Keep your message shorter than thirty seconds and you'll come off as someone who takes action rather than someone who talks about it.

Give 'Em Structure. If there are several items to address in the message, announce them right away, and then take each in turn. "There's a structure to all communications that linguists refer to as the frame, the context in which people expect to hear certain things," says Suzette Haden Elgin, Ph.D., associate professor emeritus of linguistics at San Diego State University. "Anything that breaks people out of the frame causes them to start missing the information." Nail the structure of the message by taking sixty seconds before you call to scratch out four or five bullet points. Yes, it sounds simplistic, but it can mean the difference between a lucid message and a meandering mess. It also drastically reduces the "ums" and "ers" that signal nervousness and lack of professionalism.

What to Say. During the follow-up call after your interview, you should be able to reference how a particular project mentioned during the meeting can benefit from your experience. "Otherwise your voice mail will be like every other telephone solicitation that comes in the middle of someone's dinner," says Ron Fink, managing partner of The Lewis Group, a recruiting firm specializing in the pulp and paper, printing and graphics, and banking and finance industries. Or you might say that you have some additional questions about the position. That way you can demonstrate your enthusiasm about the job and likely get a call back, says Sylvia Solorzano, a technical recruiter at Agilent Technologies in Palo Alto, California.

Pace Yourself.   In making snap judgments about which messages to attend to, people often unconsciously take linguistic cues from the caller's delivery. Speaking too slowly could mean the beginning of a long, drawn-out voice mail. Speaking too fast forces the listener to replay the message, or, more likely, to move on to the next one. Subtle phrasing can also send unwanted signals. "Women in particular often lift their intonation at the end of a sentence, as you would for a question," says Erin McKean, who edits *Verbatim*, an academic journal about language. "That can make you sound tentative and hesitant."

Say It Again.   The company already has your phone number, but you'll make it easier for the recruiter to call you back if you leave your number at the end of the message.

Network Your Way
to the Top

IT WASN'T LONG AGO THAT YOU COULD FALL OUT OF
a tree and land on a job. Now you need a living, breathing
network of contacts just to get an interview, let alone an
offer. Establishing a productive network requires constant
attention and endless creativity. Most networking advice
consists of the same timeworn clichés dished out by "career
specialists," who, you can't help noticing, sound an awful lot
like high school guidance counselors. Here you'll find the
inside dirt, the very antithesis of the kind of tired advice
that's been handed out like cafeteria Jell-O ever since your
dad was looking for a job. We've inserted you in myriad sit-
uations—the cattle-call interview, the crowded convention
hall, the cramped interview room—and supplied a list of
tips for every scenario. How? By asking the people on the

other side of the networking game—the targets, if you will—to tell us what works, what doesn't, and what to do when you finally find yourself sitting next to that managing director at the local bar.

Laying the Network

Legwork

The foundation of any network is hunting and gathering

1. Everyone reads the *Wall Street Journal.* But how about *Spatula Marketing Quarterly* or *Modern Energy Trader*? "If someone tells me he heard about my company through a trade publication, I'm particularly impressed because he's done his research," says Richard Roher, head of Chappaqua, New York–based Roher Public Relations, whose clients include Kenwood and L-3 Communications. "That's one in the plus column already."

2. Challenging the very people you want to work for shows you're not a sheep. Just make sure you're right—or at least rational. "A number of years ago, a partner here published a position paper," says Joe Shalleck, partner and branch manager at Marakon Associates, an international management-consulting firm whose clients include Boeing and Dow Chemical. "A young man saw the piece and wrote us a letter critiquing the thesis and explaining why he

thought the position was wrong. He mentioned in the letter that he was interested in our work and would like to come in and speak with the paper's author. Ten years later, he's a partner here."

3. If there's a company you want to work for, develop a fresh idea about how it might address one of the challenges it faces. Tim Dunne, a VP of business and e-business development at Nextel Communications, calls it writing your own case study: "For example, we don't actively talk about mobile advertising, but if you evaluated our press releases and asked questions of someone who works here, you'd see that we're experimenting with it. You'd see that many wireless-content companies failed last year. From all this, you'd theorize that the industry should be vocal about strategies, not stealthy." And if you told this to a manager, you'd come off as a bold, independent thinker.

4. A good contact list should contain about 250 names. Katharine Hansen, author of *A Foot in the Door: Networking Your Way into the Hidden Job Market*, says that although most people come up with about forty names during their first brainstorm, that's too few. She compares it to planning a big wedding: Make sure no one is left out. High school teachers, former college roommates, your dentist—you never know who might be a good source.

5. Hell, even religious gatherings can be full of good contacts. After getting laid off from Intellinex, a spin-

off of Ernst & Young, Michael Montgomery, a graduate of Southern Methodist University's Cox School of
Business, had an idea: ask his Bible study group,
Brothers in Christ, if anyone had any leads. "Here
were a bunch of like-minded professional men who
lived near me, had a lot of connections, and shared
my values," he says. Montgomery sent out his resumé to all eighty members, one of whom passed
along the information to his wife, who worked at
Sabre. A few days later, Montgomery came in for an
interview and landed a job as a senior sales analyst.

6. For the shy networker, similar help is available on-
line. Dozens of good websites have sprung up to
offer networking and mentoring assistance over the
Internet. These sites are great for those who aren't
naturally outgoing or feel intimidated at the
thought of one-on-one networking. Kelly Laferriere,
who's worked in interactive content at ESPN and as a
columnist for one such site, webgrrls.com, which
specializes in giving networking and mentoring advice to women working on the Web, says, "If you can
find a safe haven like webgrrls.com where the resources are available on-line, it is easy and painless
to solicit advice and knowledge from people who
want to help you."

7. Scour trade publications for executives who are
quoted; they'll be flattered when you tell them you
came across the story. During his recent job search,
Gary Hersch found a story in Phoenix's *Business Jour-*

nal about Warnick & Company, a local consulting firm and investment bank specializing in the hospitality industry—doing just the kind of work Hersch was looking for. He called Tom Marone, a managing director quoted in the story. "I asked what he did every day, did he like it, what he looks for in an employee, and would he be willing to sit down and talk," says Hersch. Marone was so impressed with Hersch's directness that he gave him three industry contacts—one of which led to an interview.

Making Contact

When and how to reach out

1. Tim Anderson figured that one good way to show an executive you're resourceful is to get access to his e-mail address. As a second-year MBA student, Anderson targeted a few companies and experimented with standard e-mail prefixes ("firstname.lastname," "firstname_lastname," and so forth) in hopes of reaching the higher-ups directly. After a slew of bounced messages from that bastard Mailer Daemon, he received more than a dozen replies straight from high-level execs.

2. If you know exactly who you want to talk to, there's no need to waste energy dreaming up an elaborate plan. Just call the person. Says Nancy Starr, a financial adviser in Merrill Lynch's private-client group:

"When I know I won't get through initially, I just leave a message. This is who I am, this is who suggested I call you, and this is what I need to know. If you're up-front and honest, people get back to you. Don't shilly-shally around trying to finagle face time. Just plow straight ahead."

3. Use the term "shilly-shally" sparingly.

4. A perfectly timed e-mail will impress the person you are talking to. Says Sonny Ajmani, a VP of strategic development in the e-commerce division at D&B (formerly Dun & Bradstreet): "Somebody sent me his résumé recently, and when he called to follow up he started off by saying, 'I've got a deal sheet. Can I send that to you?' He e-mailed it to me right then. On it were the names of more than a dozen partners, with a one-line description of what the partnership was. This kind of forethought made me feel that if he were representing D&B to potential partners, he'd be well prepared and persistent enough to open doors. In a ten-minute conversation, he did exactly what I would want him to do for a living."

5. It's generally okay to be aggressive, but sometimes it's best to chill. "I like it when people call two to three days after I've met them at an event," says Kevin McGowan, a principal at A.T. Kearney in Chicago and a University of Chicago business school grad. "What I don't like is someone who calls the next day, because I'm still trying to catch up. You'd

be surprised how many people send me e-mails the night of an event wanting to talk to me the next day."

What to Say—Exactly

A clip-and-save guide to keep in your wallet

1. You're sitting at the bar. You overhear the guy next to you mention that he works at Merrill. You would sing the complete works of Captain and Tennille naked at Disney World for a chance to work at Merrill. What do you do? "Be honest," says David Gardner, the VP of business development at AllResearch, an intelligence-gathering firm whose clients include Coca-Cola, Dell, J.P. Morgan, and Lucent. "Say, 'God, I'd love to work there. Do you enjoy it?'" That way, you put him in a position of authority, a technique Gardner calls "flattery, with taste."

2. How do you differentiate your conversation from the other 8,000 a recruiter has had that week? Personalize, personalize, personalize. She tells you she's just back from a trip? Demonstrate compassion by asking whether her heavy travel schedule is tough. Hey, recruiters are people, too.

3. From the least-favorite-question department, courtesy of Don Gamble, former director of university relations for Lucent: "Can you tell me about Lucent?"

Asking suggests laziness and ignorance—and you'd be surprised, Gamble says, how many times he hears it.

4. When an executive takes the time for an informational interview, don't just plop down your resumé and ask what you should do with your life. "I don't want to provide your inspiration," says Janet Hanson, a former Goldman Sachs vice president who now heads up Milestone Capital. "I'm not a stand-in for a therapist. I'm not an executive coach. I can use my resources to connect you to the right people, but you have to give me information. What are you good at? What do you want to do? You have to have ideas, understand trends, and be well read."

5. Few professionals have time for unsolicited phone calls seeking advice. "If somebody calls at the wrong time, you want to help, but you can't, and if you're busy, it's always the wrong time," says ESPN's Laferriere. "But if someone e-mails me first, I'm happy to provide feedback on my own time and set something up from there." An initial e-mail should be brief and to the point: Explain why you're contacting the person, what you're looking for, and how they can help you. It's a good idea to include a compelling subject line that will convince them to open your message. "Referred by _____" or "Fellow alum looking for help" might work. When you do reach them by phone, your call will be welcomed and ex-

pected, and your contact will be better prepared to help you.

6. Word choice is key when hitting up a contact for additional names. "Say, 'Who else do you think I should be talking to?' rather than 'So, do you have the names of some other good contacts?'" says Dave Tambling, a strategic-planning manager at Agilent Technologies. This can make the difference between coming across as admirably eager and arrogantly pushy.

The Art of the Mingle

Dos and don'ts of mixing with the locals

1. "I equate mingling with dating," says Tom Thivierge, director of talent acquisition for General Motors North America. "When someone approaches me, I'm going to look for eye contact and confidence. Also, that they're patient and that they waited for me to finish talking to another person."

2. Parties can be perfect networking spots, but nobody wants to feel like he's still at the office. According to Jon Piper, a recruiter at L.E.K. Consulting, which counsels Fortune 500 companies: "I'm happy to spend ten minutes at a party talking about L.E.K., but anything beyond that is excessive. Don't ask me about the nitty-gritty details of the hiring process."

Doing so suggests you don't understand the bound-
aries between work and play.

3. Don't begin every sentence with "I." It stifles conversation and makes you sound self-centered. And nobody wants to be a self-centered conversation-stifler.
Or to hire one.

4. If recruiters don't come to you, go to them. Although
Babson's F.W. Olin Graduate School of Business is
ranked in the top fifty, it doesn't always attract as
many recruiters from multinational companies as,
say, Harvard, which is a fifteen-minute drive away.
When Ildiko Kiss was a second-year at Olin, she discovered on General Mills's website that the company was hosting an information session at Harvard.
She strolled in, participated, and collected business
cards, never mentioning that she wasn't a student at
HBS—but never saying that she was. Kiss then sent
her resumé to General Mills, writing in her cover letter that she had attended the Harvard information
session and acknowledging that she was, in fact, a
Babson student. Her slightly subversive but totally
legit persistence paid off: She's now an associate
brand manager at the company.

5. Make your business card stand out from the others
that pile up in desk drawers by scribbling a note on
it just before you hand it over. "I always write something specific to our conversation," says Annie
Whitescarver, a vice president at T. Rowe Price in Bal-
timore. It could be a URL you told the person about,

for example, or your cell number. And use a red pen—it'll look like neon amid all the black type on white card stock.

6. Keep your browser fired up during all phone calls. Soon after getting his MBA, Chris Frost wanted a meeting at Microsoft. His first contact was a junior product manager who asked him to please go away. Frost saw the rejection as a toehold. He told Junior that he'd be in Seattle the first week of October and asked if they could meet. Too bad, said Junior, I'm going to be at the XYZ conference that week. Still on the phone, Frost frantically looked up the conference on the Web and was instantly in the know—"Amsterdam should be nice that time of year," he said. At that moment, the rapport seemed suddenly to improve. Frost got back in touch a few days later to say his Seattle trip had been rescheduled for the end of October. He got the meeting.

Two Ways to Sound Smart

Feel free to think of more on your own

1. Did you know that Boston Consulting Group's midtown Manhattan skyscraper is modeled after a landmark antiques shop next door? Or that UBS Warburg has a division in a Chicago office building, the Rookery, which takes its name from an emergency water

tank that stood on the site following the great fire of 1871? It doesn't take a lot of digging to unearth *Jeopardy!*-style facts about a company, and they sure make the elevator ride more interesting—and make you look that much smarter.

2. At most large corporations, the highlights of the CEO's life story are legendary. If as an outsider you can drop a line like, "Well, being the sailor that he is, Mr. Swampscott would probably love the décor in this restaurant," you've begun your approach to insiderhood.

Calling on Professors

Because their Rolodexes are made of gold

1. By the time you need a job, it's too late to start asking professors for some networking love. "The students I help have always developed a relationship with me prior to asking for help," says Olav Sorenson, assistant professor of strategy at UCLA's Anderson School.

2. Some schools foot the bill for professors and students to have lunch, a nice way to network on the administration's dime. Which, when you think about it, used to be your dime. So get your dime's worth.

3. If you're tanking a class, at least do it with a good attitude. "Students shouldn't assume that a faculty

member won't help them because they did not do well in a class," says Sorenson. "Whether I will expend effort in helping a student depends far more on whether I have enjoyed my interactions with him or her than whether he or she aced the final. The qualities for which we grade are not necessarily those that make a great employee."

4. Mention to a professor that you'll be at Thursday's keg party and that you'd love to meet him there. "Students don't realize it, but a lot of professors are just waiting for that invitation," says a marketing professor at NYU's Stern School of Business.

Resumé Game

Two tricks to put it in play

1. If a contact doesn't request a copy of your resumé, one way to get her to look at it is to ask for a quick critique. "Get over the feeling that you're imposing on the person," says a former McKinsey recruiter. "You have to be politely aggressive. Ask me to look at your resumé, and then when you go home and make the changes I suggest, e-mail me a revised copy, and ask if it's better."

2. On your resumé, highlight any clubs you belong to or hobbies that might improve your chances. They may be more important than your grades. Vito Iaia

founded the Music Business Group at Northwest-
ern's Kellogg School of Business while a student
there. The club promoted local bands, and Iaia used
it to help snare a job at an entertainment promotion
and consulting firm that handles such clients as Brit-
ney Spears and U2. At his interview, says Iaia, "the
club was a main topic of discussion."

Keeping Your Network Warm

You'll need it again and again, even when you're CEO

1. Don't call a contact only when you happen to need
   something. Maintain a dialogue a few times a year.
   "Invite him to a party, tell him you found an article he
   might like to read," says one former Goldman Sachs
   associate. "If you talk somewhat regularly, then when
   you call to ask for help, it won't be out of place."

2. Or ask for advice on something seemingly insignifi-
   cant—say, a restaurant or movie recommendation.
   Not only will this make the person feel like an authority, but it also has a built-in follow-up: You call
   back to let him know how the food was. (Hint: Even if
   it wasn't great, it was great.)

3. Cleaning out your wallet? Don't throw away a single
   business card. "A lot of people think that somebody
   they met who works in finance is of no use to them
   now that they're looking for a tech job. They're

wrong," says AllResearch's Gardner. "A network is a network. Other people move from industry to industry just as much as you might."

Polishing Your Act

A little cleverness goes a long way

1. How to look smooth, get well nourished, and score multiple job leads, all in about an hour: Invite several people you've met from the same company to lunch. As Suzanne Welch, VP of corporate marketing at Corning in Corning, New York, puts it: "One candidate recently invited me to have lunch with two other people from the company. They happened to be people I knew but who I hardly see anymore. We had a grand time. The subject turned to the student's job search and what could be done, and by the end of lunch we were taking notes about who else we could refer him to at the company. It was really a lovely, creative approach."

2. Remember people's names. When a job lead asks, "So, who else have you met in the company?" she's quizzing you. Wrong answer: "Oh, a guy in marketing—tall, kind of darkish light hair, glasses, I think."

3. Having a party? Invite all your contacts, even if you know they can't come. That way, you're sure to be on the invite list for their next shindig.

4. Never find yourself saying, "Oh, jeez, I'm all out of cards. Here, I can just write my number on the back of this video-store receipt." Always have more than you need, even when walking your dog.

5. Thank-you notes, of course, are mandatory networking tools. But if someone is kind enough to give you a referral that actually leads to a job interview or something fruitful, send a bottle of wine. "That's certainly appreciated and not out of line," says the former McKinsey recruiter. If you want to leave a more lasting impression, give a contact a copy of a recent novel you've read and inscribe it with a personal note. This is a classy move that shows you think about things other than networking.

6. If a contact helps you actually land a job, consider sending over an exotic animal or a medium-size SUV.

How to Work a Room

Perhaps one of the most underrated sources of long-lasting networking contacts is the business conference. Sure, the name tags are dorky, and the chances you'll meet your next business partner are probably slim. But if you show up and talk your game, there's a decent chance that someone you meet will know someone who knows someone who knows someone—who just might be your next business partner. For advice on how to get the most from a conference, we suggest you follow along below as one networking pro plies her magic.

It's 6:50 A.M. at an early-riser business-and-technology conference at the Museum of Science in Boston. A model of Skylab hangs from the high ceiling of the upper concourse, giving the room a dreamy feeling. The attendees, a mix of about 750 entrepreneurs, techies, and venture capitalists, have come to scout clients, money, and jobs.

Diane Darling is hunting clients. If there's such a thing as a professional networker, it's Darling, a business school lecturer and founder of Effective Networking, a company that trains business leaders and MBA students. As the conference begins, she straightens her name tag, pops an Altoid, and strides into the crowd.

Don't Go in Cold.   A week before the event, Darling asked one of the sponsors for a list of attendees. "That way I could do a little research on people I want to meet and use that information to break the ice with them," she explains. "Are these people entrepreneurs? CEOs? VCs? I try to know as much as I can about the crowd before going."

Travel Light.   Darling wears a tasteful red jacket. "There are a bazillion blue suits here. I stand out in this jacket—but not in a bad way." She carries only a leather portfolio, about twice the size of a wallet, with two pockets: one for business cards coming in, the other for cards going out. No fumbling.

Walk the Walk.   She moves through the concourse confidently, smiling. "Young people tend to act like beggars when they schmooze for jobs. But that sends the wrong signal. Powerful people come to these events because they want to meet other skilled, talented people. So carry yourself accordingly. Don't fold your arms. Look like you're having a good time."

Start with Breakfast.   Darling's first stop is the long breakfast buffet—but not because she's hungry. "People tend to be very accessible around the food. Talking and eating go together. It's a great way to get started at an event," she says, carrying her orange juice in her left hand so she can shake with her right.

Who's Who.   To scope out the crowd and pick her targets from the hundreds of attendees, Darling circles the large room once, quickly scanning name tags. "Don't read name tags while talking to people. Always maintain eye contact." Besides, sideways glances make you look furtive and shifty.

Approach VIPs First.   Darling darts over to one of the morning's guest speakers, a Harvard Business School professor, fifteen minutes before his presentation starts. "Keynote speakers love to talk and can be great contacts, but after they give their speeches they're always swamped."

Spot the Lone Wolves.   The room is crowded, so Darling next looks for people who are standing alone. "It's harder to integrate into a group. Besides, individual contact is best; one-on-one makes for the most effective networking. Just make sure you smile as you approach."

"And You Are?"   She approaches a man near the podium and very briefly tells him why she's at the conference. "Hi. I'm here because I founded Effective Networking. We train people how to build their businesses and careers," she says to the guy. "My name is Diane Darling." She says her name at the end so he's more likely to remember it.

Press the Flesh.   When meeting others, she's the first to extend her hand. "It's an old protocol, a sign that you're eager to interact," she says later. Also: Make sure to shake hands good-bye, especially if you're a woman. "It's not as natural a part of a woman's repertoire as it is of a man's, so a good-bye handshake will be memorable."

Feel 'Em Out.   While talking with strangers, Darling asks open-ended questions to determine quickly whether they'll be of any help. "Don't go into a polished twenty-second commercial about yourself. Real leaders are curious. You're trying to pass the test as a personable human being first and as a talented job candidate second."

Card Exchange.   Darling asks everyone she meets for a business card before she offers her own. "It's less presumptuous."

Get an Introduction.   After traversing the room twice, she spots the conference moderator, a player in the Boston media world. He's alone drinking coffee, but rather than approach him solo, she enlists a mutual acquaintance to give her an introduction. "An intro is like an implicit endorsement, and the next time we meet, there will be that association and that context."

Give and Take.　The moderator mentions that he's looking to get in touch with a professor at MIT whom Darling happens to know. She offers to make an introduction. "Always try to be a connector, the person who brings people together," she says. This not only makes Darling look tapped in but may also make the moderator want to return her favor.

That's a Wrap.　After three hours, Darling has talked with around two dozen new contacts. She leaves the conference with plans to call these leads in the next week. "Remember, you're not there to close deals or get a job. You're there to get the right to follow up with a phone call or a meeting over coffee. Even one contact like that makes the whole day worthwhile."

The Ultimate Recruiting Playbook (Business School Special)

From start to finish, the campus recruiting process is loaded with established guidelines, deadlines, schedules, and rules. But beyond the advice doled out by those stale how-to books, there's a vast pool of unwritten knowledge handed down with a wink by benevolent recruiters and job-search veterans. These nuggets of wisdom and guerrilla tactics are off the record and between the lines—and could mean the difference between coming in for a second interview and coming in second place. But to get the goods, you have to know the right people. We do. In fact, many of our recruiting experts have such high positions that they wouldn't let their names be used. You'll soon see why.

Avoiding Rookie Mistakes

1. Need to call a recruiter? Do it before nine or after five. That way, you won't get her assistant. (Assistants almost never make hiring decisions.) If no one answers, just leave a message. Don't hang up and call back five more times. Ever heard of caller ID?

2. At business school, make friends with a second-year who's already received offers from companies you want to work for. Why? Because many recruiters ask new hires who the stars of the incoming class are, and you want yours to be the name they drop. Don't disguise your motives. "It's perfectly within protocol for a first-year to ask a second-year to have a beer or a cup of coffee to talk about a company," says one NYU Stern grad. "If I like you, I'll definitely pass your name along, but don't e-mail me your resumé out of the clear blue and expect me to submit it to the company."

3. Calling distant relatives or friends of friends of friends to network is a good move, but don't spend more than two sentences explaining your connection to the person. "Within thirty seconds, I should know that you're good for the job because you're at the top of your class, not because you used to play on my kid's soccer team," says one recruiter for a major bank.

4. Companies that recruit on B-school campus adhere to rigid schedules—but that's no reason you should. "A month before they hit campus, write a letter or make a call to each company's rep to introduce yourself," says Antoinette Chambers, former director of MBA career services at the University of Tennessee. "They'll be impressed with your interest and initiative, and when the recruiters show up, I guarantee they'll remember your name."

5. From Jose Andino, former human resources manager at CNBC.com, who sees ten to fifteen recruits a week: "People spend more time investigating the type of house they're going to buy than the company that's hopefully going to help them buy it. And the ones who do conduct research usually confine it to the Internet. These days, that's not enough. You'd be surprised how much information you can get from calling a receptionist or chatting with a security guard—they often know more than you might expect about the company culture, and they're usu-

ally willing to talk. The first question to ask: Do people at this company generally seem happy? You'll get a lot of mileage out of that one."

6. At most companies, you're pitching yourself to two audiences: human resources and the hiring manager. So prepare two resumés, advises DeAnne Rosenberg, president of DeAnne Rosenberg, Inc., a career consultancy in Wareham, Massachusetts. One should list your credentials and experience; the other should emphasize your ability to learn. HR is simply trying to fill an order—two MBAs with X, Y, and Q experience, Rosenberg says. In a single glance at your resumé, they should see that you have X, Y, and Q, so go ahead and detail your course selection within your marketing major. Get more creative with the resumé for the hiring manager. Show how you used your marketing knowledge to create a new branding concept for the last company you worked for. She's interested in how prospective employees think and how they've taken initiative.

7. At every possible opportunity, quantify your accomplishments. This makes what you're saying instantly credible and tangible. Saying "Acquired ten new accounts for my brokerage last year, which ranked me first in the group" is much better than "Led group in account acquisitions." Why? Recruiters are constantly comparing candidates with one another, and

they'll subconsciously associate your name with the phrase "ten new accounts."

The Cattle Calls

1. Always go to the company's presentation, no matter how much you already know about the firm. When an interviewer asks if you were there—and they will ask—your "Yes" will be an honest answer. Says a former associate at one of the biggest banks on the Street: "I only missed one, and sure enough, I was asked about it in the interview. It was definitely a smudge on my record."

2. Following a corporate presentation, don't approach the big-deal partner to chat her up and get her card; thirty other people will be doing precisely that. Instead, peg one of her subordinates, who likely has a hand in the early stages of the process. "You'll get quality time with a person who counts right now rather than a quick handshake from a big shot you won't be dealing with until later," says a former recruiting-team leader for a major strategic consultant.

3. At large recruiting events, swallow your sartorial pride and wear the damn name tag. If they aren't preprinted and you have to make your own, write your last name twice as large as your first. Then stick the thing over your right breast. That way, when you

reach out your hand to shake, your name will jump directly into the person's line of sight.

4. Recruiter: *What would you like to drink? You: Um, what kind of beer is there? No wait, maybe I'll have a gin and—well, actually—*Wrong, wrong, wrong. When it comes to alcohol consumption, know what you want to order. It doesn't matter whether it's a Scotch or a spritzer, make it sound like you've asked for it a thousand times before. Then don't ask for it more than twice again all night.

5. If you can, mention a recent book or article that the hiring manager probably hasn't read. Pique his interest in it. This creates a natural follow-up opportunity—send him the article the next day along with a (very) short note.

The Interview

1. The rule of thumb for addressing prospective employers: "For someone no more than two levels above the position you want, use his or her first name," says one Silicon Alley CEO. "For someone three levels or more up, use 'Mr.' or 'Ms.' until they instruct you otherwise." Never use "Homeslice" or "Sweetie."

2. If you don't immediately know the answer to a question during a case interview, look down while you think of something to say. The natural tendency is to

look up, but politicians and other seasoned public speakers are coached to stare at the floor. It gives the appearance of being deep in thought.

3. From an adjunct professor of marketing at a top twenty B-school: "In a second interview, ask the recruiter why you were selected. This, of course, takes some finesse. Don't ask in a 'Why me? I'm not worthy' sort of way. Just be curious and confident. This will get your inquisitor talking about you—and let you know exactly what you should be talking to her about."

4. Acceptable reasons for not being available on the first date the recruiter proposes for a second interview: wedding (yours only); concussion (yours only).

5. Whether it's asked during a "friendly" recruiting dinner or in a Super Saturday grilling, the hobby question is always a trick. Don't talk about the last novel you read or your praying mantis collection. These are solo activities. "Companies want team players," explains the president of a small high-tech recruiting firm. "Talk about something that demonstrates your ability to work with others." Even if skiing's your sport, turn it into a group activity by mentioning how you organized nine friends to go in on a condo last winter and hit the slopes en masse.

6. From Danielle Martin, the human resources manager at BTS USA, a management-consulting company in Stamford, Connecticut: "In the final stage of our re-

cruiting process, each candidate gives a brief presentation on a company of her choice in front of five consultants in our firm. One candidate, who had just been introduced to the group for the first time, addressed each person by name when answering questions. To me that showed she paid attention to detail, and that she could keep her composure when interrupted by questions—both skills we look for." This goes for the entire recruiting process, of course. When someone asks who else you've met at the company (you can count on this), use the clever mnemonic devices you've created, and rattle off seventeen names as if reciting your home phone number.

Interview Aftermath

1. "Save your best question for right after an interview, when, say, you're being walked to the elevator," says Amy Giering, a graduate of NYU Stern. "The interviewer will be more focused on your question, because she's not thinking about the ten things she has to ask you." It'll also show the interviewer that you're uncommonly inquisitive and that you think well on your feet. Plus, it makes an excellent final impression.

2. Never call a recruiter from a cell phone. Ever.

3. "Dear Mr. _____: The purpose of this letter is to thank you for the opportunity to interv—" Whoa,

Officious One, stop right there. Everyone writes cookie-cutter thank-you letters. More effective is the "influence letter," in which the candidate makes all the carefully articulated points that he didn't make in the interview. In one page, restate your most relevant qualifications. Then advance the discussion you had by taking it one step further: "I was thinking about your question concerning the plant in Mexico, and I think one solution might be—"

4. If you're waiting for callbacks from prospective employers, instruct your housemates to say politely that you're either:

   A. at the library

   B. out shopping your business plan

   C. not back from Davos yet

5. Instruct said housemates never to use the following words or phrases:

   A. probation officer

   B. Tequiza

   C. sandbox

6. True story from a recent SMU B-school grad: "I was dead set on getting a job with Towers Perrin, but the company said it was only hiring Ivy Leaguers and students from other schools in the Northeast. So I flew to Chicago on spring break—with no appointment scheduled—and walked into the company's headquarters wearing my best suit. I told the receptionist in the vaguest of terms that I was in the

building 'on business' and wanted to see if I could talk to the managing director. I actually got through and met one of the partners. A few weeks later, I got the job." Moral: Do whatever it takes.

7. True story from a Wharton grad: "I was at a career conference at Deloitte Consulting, and as I was leaving, I noticed the guy I had interviewed with a couple of days earlier standing out front. He was trying to hail a cab at five o'clock on a Friday, and obviously having no luck. I had driven to the event, so I sprinted five blocks to my car, pulled up in front of him, and offered him a lift. He was trying to catch a train, so he jumped in. I chatted him up the whole ride. A week later I got an offer." Moral: Do whatever it takes.

8. Let's say you're at the racetrack and you've got $72.50 riding on horse number four, a five-to-one shot that's neck-and-neck with another horse. So you're rooting for the four horse. Good. Now imagine you've got $100,000 on that horse. Suddenly you're rooting for your pony to win with every fiber of your being. Is that how much you want this job? That's what a prospective employer should think.

Networking on Uncle Sam's Dime

Tax time—not a season that typically conjures up images of governmental beneficence. But for anyone who does even a little job searching, April 15 may feel like bonus time. Lunch with a contact, a cab ride to an interview, and drinks afterward come with the territory, but those bills can add up fast. The good news: In many cases, Uncle Sam will help pay the tab.

"So many people come in and say, 'I didn't think I could deduct that,'" says Shelly Jacobson-Taylor, owner of New York tax-prep boutique SJ Associates, who's helped hundreds of young professionals tally up their deductions. "They don't realize what's coming to them."

The IRS looks at it this way: A legitimate expense is something that's specific to finding a job—and that you wouldn't use in your personal life. Also, only expenses that exceed 2 percent of your adjusted gross income are eligible for deduction. This works out well for students, most of whom don't have an entire year of income under their belts. A second-year MBA student who made $20,000 over the summer and ran up $2,400 in expenses while interviewing can write off a tidy two grand.

One big catch: To take any deductions, you must be seeking employment in the same trade you've been working in. "Someone who worked at AT&T and is now looking to go into banking can't write off job-hunting expenses," says Maggie Doedtman, senior tax specialist for H&R Block.

And finally, receipts. The IRS requires that you submit them to document your job-search efforts. So save them. Below, a few other rules of the game:

Travel. If the primary purpose of a trip is job searching, then all airfare, train tickets, rental cars, taxis, Sherpa fees—even the mileage on your own car—are fully deductible.

Lodging. Write off hotel stays, but only during the days when it's essential that you be in town. Room charges for the night before your interview are deductible, but those for the three nights that you hang around afterward are not.

Food and Drink. Write off half the cost of all meals and cocktails that pertain directly to your search. Lunch with a third cousin who's a VP at Intel? Take off 50 percent. Martinis with an old roommate who now works at Merrill? Same deal, as long as the meetings were business oriented—at least through the first round.

Briefcase. Sorry, no. While it may be a tool of the trade, it's not considered absolutely necessary for a job hunt.

Clothing. Clown suit for the circus tryout, yes. Hugo Boss suit, no. If specific clothing is required for the job, it's deductible. But the feds argue that an interview suit could also be useful in your personal life. "I can't tell you how many people buy a suit for an interview thinking they can deduct it," says Jacobson-Taylor.

Resumés. All printing, photocopying, and mailing costs for your resumé are deductible. Yes, that includes FedEx.

Long-Distance Calls.   Yep, as long as they can be tied to your job hunt.

PDA.   Although you pack it with contacts and leads, the answer, unfortunately, is a palms-down no. But, says Doedtman, "after you get the job, you can probably deduct it as a business expense."

Dining for Dollars

Just for a moment, put yourself in the wing tips of a young exec named Phil who was about to embark on the biggest power lunch of his life. "I was trying to convince the head of PR for a major TV network to consult on one of our projects, so I set up a lunch with him at a tony restaurant," he remembers. Phil arrived early and secured what he considered to be a choice table—a deuce in the back that allowed for quiet, serious conversation. "The guy showed up, took one look at me sitting in the corner, and said, 'What the hell is this? Siberia? I want to be where the action is!'" The maître d' hustled them to a table in the middle of the room. As for Phil? "I felt like a kid," he says. "The lunch was over before it started."

Whether you're trying to hire a hotshot or land a job, you're likely to find yourself at some point doing lunch. At a restaurant, however, a table's location can speak louder than any big idea; you can order the finest wine yet still manage to make a poor impression; the wait staff can interrupt at the most inopportune time. It's enough to unnerve even a seasoned pro. And since only one person can wield the power at a power lunch, here's a menu of tips to ensure that that person will be you.

Home-Field Advantage

The perfect power meal actually starts months in advance. "One rule about power is that you always want to put the other person on your territory," says Robert Greene, author of *The 48 Laws of Power*, a compilation of aphorisms about strength and guile in the business world. "Choose a place you're familiar with, preferably one where the other person has never been." There's no question that becoming a fixture helps from a strategic point of view. "If you're a regular, the waiter says, 'Hello, Mr. So-and-So,'" explains Tim Zagat, publisher of the Zagat surveys. "You feel comfortable that the bill won't get presented to your guest, or better yet, won't be presented at all," a silent clue to your guests that the restaurant considers you trustworthy.

As for the spot itself, hip is one thing, but it's best to steer clear of those velvet-corded restaurants packed to the gills with glitterati. "Those places are going to be more hot on themselves than on you," Zagat says. "You want to know that when you get there you won't be standing at the bar for forty-five minutes."

Becoming a regular takes time, but not as much as you might think. Most people eat out once a week anyway, so rein in variety and build a rapport at a single restaurant. Go Mondays and Tuesdays, when the staff will have time to remember a name and a face. Introduce yourself to the manager when you arrive ("I've heard great things about your food"), and ask for a few suggestions. Have a good experience with a particular waiter? Request him when you make the next reservation. Always tip at least 20 percent and, once a month, hand the maître d' a twenty. After a few visits, offer to buy the kitchen a round when they knock off. As Anthony Bourdain, chef at the New York City bistro Les Halles, made clear in his best-seller *Kitchen Confidential*, cooks are notoriously underappreciated and often enjoy a nip. A gesture like that could lift you out of the ranks of anonymity. If you ask the chef to prepare his favorite dishes on occasion, he might stop by the table to see how everything was. In the eyes of your tablemates, nothing can make you look more important.

The Seat of Power

If you end up at a truly awful table—those by the kitchen door or bathroom—it will cast a pall over your business lunch. The rear is generally where diners go to die: The ratio of music to background noise is fatally screwed up, and servers are an endangered species. Worse, the lack of people to watch almost encourages the eye to pick up on the small crack along the wall or a spot the broom missed—not the tone to set for wheeling and dealing. What makes a good table? If the meeting's about talk, sit on the periphery, where the energy is still palpable but diners have no problem hearing one another. If it's less about a specific deal and more about goodwill, sit in the middle, where the energy is high and the people-watching's easy. (Learning the numbers of a few key tables will eliminate guesswork and make you sound like an insider when booking a reservation.)

At the table itself, have your guest sit with his back to the door so he won't be distracted by people coming in. With long group tables, the power seats are at each end and in the middle. "The worst place to sit is next to the seat at the end," says Mark Mazzarella, a San Diego attorney and coauthor of *Put Your Best Foot Forward*, a primer on how actions are read by others. "It makes you look like the boss's underling."

In the Company of Menu

The biggest mistakes at a power lunch come when it's time to eat. Too often, the host is afraid of interrupting a good conversation to order. But if you don't, you can totally throw off the meal's timing. "People get too caught up in conversation," says Kristine Larsson, a waitress at D'Amico Cucina, a Minneapolis hot spot. "Then all of a sudden the conversation stops and they're crazed with hunger, but the waitress is gone, and you have twenty minutes until the food arrives." To minimize the interruption, ask the server to bring a few appetizers for the table while placing the drink order.

As far as menu choices go, a basic principle of power lies in mirroring your guest's requests. Subconsciously, this puts him at ease, and—who knows?—might make him more willing to divulge contacts to you. If he asks for a vodka on the rocks, it's better to order a cocktail than a beer. If he orders the pork chops, don't select a salad, which can send a signal that you think you have more self-control than he does. That said, no one wants to dine with an automaton: If a guest orders the steak au poivre and you were going to order the steak au poivre, go for sirloin. Otherwise it looks like you're a spineless kiss-up.

Getting Down to Business

At a power lunch, confidence and composure are everything. To that end, ignore the bread. The tearing, buttering, and unavoidable crumbs undercut the poise you want to project. Take a piece, but let it die on your plate. Likewise, drink slowly—quick, short sips imply nervousness—and let the menu sit idle a few minutes before cracking it.

"To project authority and power, sit forward on your chair, with a little lean over the table and your hands out in front of you," Mazzarella says. "Square your shoulders to the other person, and try not to disengage visually." In fact, err on the side of staring too long. While maintaining eye contact 60 to 70 percent of the time works in personal conversations, doing so 70 to 80 percent is expected in business conversations, according to Mazzarella.

When it comes to conversation, do a bit of opposition research on your companion, advises Charles Sacarello of Charles & Associates, a New York–based image-consulting firm. "Get a few personal details about him beforehand," he says. "Find out his interests, his hobbies. Asking about them will make him relax." Also, avoid "why" questions, which put people on the defensive, as does correcting a guest's responses or making suggestions.

By simply listening, you will not only get information but also gain an edge. "Always say less than necessary," explains Greene, *48 Laws'* author. Avoid the tendency to fill conversational gaps—your guest will be compelled to deal with them and may inadvertently give up bits of information in the rush to avoid an awkward moment. "It's like chess, and the person who talks more puts himself in a strange and vulnerable position," Greene says.

At many a business lunch, the most awkward moment of all comes at the transition from small talk to business talk. Avoid this by mentioning what prompted the invitation early on. "If you don't," Mazzarella says, "you talk and talk for an hour and a half, and all of a sudden the check's there and you're bringing up this larger subject." He advises broaching the purpose of the meeting with a thank-you at the get-go, right after the handshake, and quickly following it by showing interest in your guest's business. Then, with all the chess play and strategy out of the way, you can sit back and enjoy your dessert. You will have earned it.

Get on Board

Who wouldn't want to serve on a company's board of directors? Your decisions move markets, people return your calls, and you get to hobnob with corporate honchos. For a twenty-nine-year-old professional with a few years of work experience at a top-notch firm, this proposition is typically . . . way out of reach.

The exception is nonprofit boards. America's 1.4 million nonprofits received some $174 billion in contributions in 1998, and unlike for-profit firms, which generally give board seats only to older, more-seasoned executives, nonprofits often welcome young and savvy businesspeople. Why? They're not only eager, they also often have valuable management expertise and take the job more seriously than big-name figureheads.

The Benefits

So what does board membership do for you? Beyond contributing to a good cause, landing a spot can bolster a resumé, provide real-world management experience, and fill a PalmPilot with killer job contacts.

Richard Fitzgerald knows something about contacts. In 1998, Fitzgerald was selling LexisNexis subscriptions to law firms while pursuing his MBA at Loyola Marymount, in Los Angeles. His seventy-hour weeks provided little time for traditional networking. But at a meeting of his campus entrepreneurs' club, he met Ann Christie Gusiff, founder of Clothes the Deal, a charity that donates business wear to underprivileged people trying to enter the job market. "I wanted to make a difference, but I also wanted to further my career," says Fitzgerald. "Clothes the Deal was the perfect opportunity to do both."

Fitzgerald held regular clothes drives, and Gusiff, impressed by his enthusiasm and smarts, invited him to join Clothes the Deal's board. Suddenly, clients who wouldn't return his calls about LexisNexis were eager to talk about Clothes the Deal. Over time, discussions about old overcoats led to conversations about the news service, and then to new business.

Fitzgerald's board duties had him brainstorming with the CEO of Merrit Publishing as well as vice presidents for ViewSonic Corp. and the J. Paul Getty Trust. "I now have contacts I can tap into if I want to make a career move," he says.

That's a benefit Tom Riley, of the Philanthropy Roundtable, an association of charitable donors, has seen again and again. "Many boards have members who students might not otherwise have an opportunity to work with until later in their careers," he says. In other words, joining a nonprofit board is a way to cut to the head of the line.

There are other benefits, as well. Learning board-room etiquette now provides the training for a big-league seat ten years down the road. And it never hurts to be able to say: "I'd love to, but I've got a board meeting to attend."

Find the Right Board

So you've got a warm heart and an ulterior motive. Now what? There's always the obvious approach: Find a non-profit you like and contact a board member. Or, say you're looking to land a spot at Kleiner Perkins. Read the partner bios to see if they serve on any boards, then volunteer.

If you're at B-school, a great source to guide your search is probably right on campus. "Professors often know the nonprofit leaders in the community. They can point to prominent people on accessible boards," says Donna Fishman of the Community Service Society of New York. Fishman also advises checking the alumni association for high-flying grads affiliated with, say, a local Habitat for Humanity chapter.

"Once the other board members see that you're sharp and dedicated, you'll build a link and they'll naturally want to help you," explains David Meierding, a student at Kellogg and a board member of Women and Youth Supporting Each Other. "It's certainly worked for me."

CHAPTER 4

Ace the Interview

IT'S YOUR BIG DEBUT. YOUR MOMENT IN THE SUN.

Your chance to knock 'em dead—or get carried out on a stretcher. The interview, because of its do-or-die, now-or-never, rubber-meets-the-road realities, looms large in the minds of job-seekers. As well it should. Blow an interview, and you may well have wasted months of tireless networking, hours of painstaking preparation, and at least one trip to the dry cleaner.

Don't let the pressure get to you, though. Once you understand what's really going on in that room—the nuances, the details, the subtexts—you stand a good chance of prevailing. We've broken the interview down, put its parts under the microscope, scrutinized them, weighed them, measured them, and, finally, reassembled them, all to help you get past the angst and on to the prize.

The Anatomy of an Interview

What does an interview look like from the interviewer's chair? Which answers impress? Which comments annoy? What shoots you dead? Here, some shrewd tips and subtle tricks from top recruiters, career consultants, and psychologists.

Six Tips for the First Two Minutes

Because nothing matters more than a first impression

1. Everyone knows not to be late for an interview. But recruiters say arriving early is just as bad—in fact, showing up even ten minutes ahead of time may irritate them. Why? You will interrupt whatever they're doing ("Ms. Jenkins, your next appointment is here"), which can sow a seed of resentment. It also sends a message: You are an amateur, both overeager and overworried about being late. Arrive no more than five minutes before the interview. If you find yourself there earlier than that, look for a bench outside, read the newspaper, and . . . floss or something.

2. While you're waiting for the interviewer to greet you, always remain standing. "You don't want the very first thing the interviewer sees to be you getting your things in order and adjusting your clothing," says Anne Warfield, president of Impression Management Professionals, a Minneapolis-based

career-consulting firm whose clients include 3M and American Express.

3. Sociolinguists at Stanford University have discovered that what we say accounts for a mere 7 percent of a person's first impression of us, whereas our body language constitutes 55 percent. In case they're right, hold your briefcase or bag in your left hand and keep the right one hanging loosely at your hip, ready to shake hands.

4. When speaking with the recruiter's assistant, use her name. A simple, respectful "Thanks, Denise" could mean a kind word from Denise to her boss later.

5. Be prepared for the potentially awkward moment when you and the recruiter walk into a conference room for the interview and there are more than two chairs. If she hasn't yet taken a seat, rest your hand on one of the chairs and ask, "Is this a good place for me to sit?" If the interviewer has already set up shop, "choose the seat directly across from her," says Michele Mamet, associate director of university relations at Bristol-Myers Squibb. "If the table is round, sit next to her, but move away so you can look her dead in the eye."

6. The interviewer may well kick things off with the dreaded "Tell me about yourself." If he asks, you gotta tell him. But since your best overall MO is to release information about yourself in strategic deployments throughout the interview, resist the urge to

dump it all at once. John Worth, director of career consulting at the University of Virginia's Darden School and a former recruiter at Deloitte Consulting, advises rehearsing a sixty-second commercial spot that summarizes your responsibilities at your last job, capped by your reasons for pursuing this position. Begin this last part with the phrase "But what I really want to do is . . . "

Three Rules for Breaking the Ice

The wrong small talk can hurt you

1. Family photos can be great conversation starters—if you choose your comments wisely. (You: "Your mother has a great smile." Him: "That's my wife.") "Making assumptions about the people in the pictures is dangerous," says Debra Fine, founder of The Fine Art of SmallTalk, a Denver firm that teaches conversation skills to executives at companies like IBM and Wells Fargo. "If a picture is facing you, it's fair game, but be vague: 'What a great picture. Where was it taken?'"

2. Think before cracking jokes. "The safest, most effective kind of humor is self-deprecating," says Albert Chen, executive director of graduate programs at Kaplan Test Prep, "but this is one situation where you don't want to put yourself down."

3. Never talk about traffic, sports, or the weather. You don't want to be the eleventh automaton that day to say, "Wow, sure is hot."

Five Moves That Show You're a Pro

This is no time for subtlety

1. Have an agenda. "One of the biggest mistakes people make is thinking the goal is simply to answer the questions that are asked," says J. Daniel Plants, a managing director at J.P. Morgan Chase. "Sure, you have to answer their questions, but the best candidates know how to steer the conversation where they want it to go."

2. Wanna be an executive? Your first step is to sit like one. Powerful people have no qualms about taking up a lot of space. Sit up straight in the middle of the chair, with one arm on the armrest and the other on the table. You'll instantly look and feel more confident and in control.

3. Tell a story. "There should be a theme that runs through every answer," says a former recruiter for McKinsey & Co. "Maybe it's 'I'm creative.' Whatever your story, tell it clearly and succinctly. Tailor an explanation of your strengths and weaknesses to support it."

4. Admit past mistakes in a way that shows you learned something. "Let's say you once did some-

thing that a client wanted but that wasn't what your boss wanted," says Joni Johnston, a psychologist and the CEO of WorkRelationships, a management training company whose clients include Nokia and Ericsson. "Explain that while your instinct was to please the client—a good instinct—you learned that your manager's wishes are most important."

5. Obey the rule of three. Have three points to drive home and an anecdote to support each one. If you're applying for a sales position, maybe the points are: "I've sold before," "I have great contacts," and "I understand this business." "This may seem obvious," says the former McKinsey recruiter, "but you'd be surprised how many people come in with zero structure to what they're saying. If you've thought ahead about what you want to communicate, an interviewer notices."

Three Signs You're Losing Control

And three ways to get it back

1. If a recruiter asks more than once whether you have any questions, chances are she's already formed an opinion about you and is trying to wrap it up. "Ask for a glass of water," says Jackie Johnson, manager of MBA recruiting for the investment bank Dresdner Kleinwort Wasserstein. Dramatic? Perhaps. "But it'll

help you collect your thoughts," she says. It also creates the impression that the interview has a first half and a second half. Shine in the second half, and you've got a chance. "I've definitely had people who I wasn't sure about at first but who made a strong comeback," says Johnson.

2. Should you draw a complete blank to a question, ask the interviewer to rephrase it. "People are scared to ask this, because they think they'll look stupid," says Joni Johnston. "That's not true. And even if you do understand the question, you'll have a moment to collect your thoughts while they rephrase it."

3. "There's a time in every person's interviewing process when they're rambling along and they suddenly say to themselves, 'I have no idea where I'm going with this,'" says Gail Wasserman, a former VP of public affairs at American Express and managing partner at the Maloney Group, a New York management-consulting firm. "Pause. Check in, and say, 'Have I answered your question?'"

Deal Breakers

Seven things recruiters hate and why they hate them

1. Taking notes during an interview is fine, but keep your pen holstered unless absolutely necessary. Excessive scribbling indicates an inability to think on

your feet. "When I hire somebody, I'm looking for them to be able to represent me at meetings," says Wasserman, "not take dictation."

2. Shoes that aren't shined. Details matter.

3. INTERVIEWER: "We're opening a new office in Charlottesville."

CANDIDATE: "Oh, I've heard it's great there."

INTERVIEWER: "Really? I'm from there. What have you heard about it?"

CANDIDATE: [*Pauses. Starts to cry.*]

If you don't mean it, don't say it. "If I mention that travel is a big part of the job, and someone immediately says that they love to travel, well, I hate that," says Rob Britton, a PricewaterhouseCoopers consultant. A pointed follow-up question will show you're not simply spitting out what you think he wants to hear.

4. Some candidates have their rap so well practiced that instead of responding to specific questions, they churn out prepackaged answers, no matter what the interviewer asks. "It's frustrating when people don't answer the question because they didn't listen to it," says Bristol-Myers Squibb's Mamet. "Don't just pull out your favorite response. It's easy for us to tell when it's rehearsed."

5. "Never swear during an interview," says a former Goldman Sachs recruiter. "I can only assume you'd do it in the first meeting with a client, too, and I can't take that risk."

6. Answering questions the way everybody else does. "If I ask, 'What's your biggest weakness?' don't say, 'I pay too much attention to detail,'" advises Mark Golin, a senior VP of creative services at AOL. "People don't realize that the recruiter has done this 400 more times than they have. If you stop and think about that, your answers will change—they'll become what they should be: unique."

7. There's standing out from the pack because you're unique, and then there's standing out because you blare your trombone louder than everyone else just to make noise. "I was once scheduling a second interview for lunch, and I suggested a restaurant," remembers one media executive. "The candidate said, 'No, I don't like the food there.' I could tell he wanted to rebuff my choice just to prove he could. The interview was over before it started."

Tactics for the Last Thirty Seconds

How to leave them begging for more

1. When the interviewer utters these five words, "Do you have any questions?" (and he will), don't make one up on the spot just to ask something. Prepare two good questions about the position or the firm—the answers to which cannot be found on the website. A great final question leaves a great final impression.

2. If you don't, in fact, have any questions, spare your-
    self an awkward moment by saying, "Do you have
    any unanswered questions about my qualifications?"
3. Take a business card. Obvious, right? Sheryl Colyer,
    director of global human resources at Citigroup
    Asset Management, says the worst mistake candi-
    dates make when sending thank-you notes is mis-
    spelling the name of the interviewer.
4. Four out of five candidates recommend a stiff Stoli
    and tonic after any interview.

Size Up Your Interviewer in Sixty Seconds

Knowing who you're talking to is half the battle. Interviewing consultant Anne Warfield has helped young professionals land jobs at firms like Qwest and 3M by coaching them
to tailor their pitch to an interviewer's personality. Here, she
divulges how to identify the four most common types of interviewers—and how to position yourself for each one.

The Analyzer

How to spot him: A Carter-administration-era tie. He
    walks through your job history to make sure every
    month is accounted for.
What matters to him: The way he sees it, your memory
    of the details of past positions is a measure of the
    care with which you'll do this job.

Winning move: Include at least one number—a stat, a date—in each answer. Speak slowly.

Losing move: Joking around or spilling personal information.

The Networker

How to spot her: She charges into the room, probably late, chattering away. She dresses boldly—a bright shirt or trendy glasses.

What matters to her: That you hear and remember *every word she says.*

Winning move: The Networker interrupts you, so keep your answers short. Show energy and enthusiasm.

Losing move: Offering detailed explanations of the minutiae of your career.

The Producer

How to spot him: He makes intense eye contact, shakes firmly, and grills you like a drill sergeant. Brooks Brothers all the way.

What matters to him: Your understanding of hierarchy and power—especially his.

Winning move: Play it straight. Answer questions directly, with one or two supporting facts, and move on.

Losing move: Digressing or equivocating. The Producer hates wasting time.

The Connector

> *How to spot her:* A relaxed gait and a warm smile. She falls all over herself offering water or coffee and trying to make you comfortable.
>
> *What matters to her:* Whether or not you'll click with others in the department.
>
> *Winning move:* Focus on your ability to work with a team. She wants to hear "we," not "I."
>
> *Losing move:* Bragging. And don't talk about "confronting" a problem or "aggressively" seeking a solution.

Every Second Counts

Below, two veteran recruiters from Morgan Stanley and Booz Allen Hamilton provide a minute-by-minute breakdown of how an interview[1] is structured—and what a recruiter looks for at every stop along the way.

The Introduction

During the crucial opening minutes, the interviewer is sizing you up as a person, as opposed to a faceless resumé. Your ability to engage in small talk and your ease when meeting new people are at a premium. Don't launch into a detailed summary of your qualifications right away—that

---

[1]Based on a first- or second-round interview that typically lasts between thirty and fifty minutes.

comes next. (Note: If it's been five minutes and you're still talking about the construction outside the office, gradually steer the conversation toward your track record.)

The Fit

The interviewer is now assessing how your experience fits the company's needs. "Don't recite your job history," says the Morgan Stanley recruiter. "Use your most recent job to talk about the future." Begin dropping clues that you understand the company's culture and business. Mention, for instance, that you have friends in the industry, and comment on the company's most recent earnings report before you're asked about it.

The Test

This is when the interviewer sees how you handle pressure. At a bank, you may be asked to sell the recruiter on a stock of your choice (figure about ten minutes). For a consulting gig, it's case study time (twenty to thirty minutes). That said, not every consulting interview includes a case; if you're twenty minutes in and there's no sign of one, there probably won't be. Don't sweat it.

The Differentiation

Here's where you leave a great lasting impression. Two strategies: Ask a couple of smart questions, or work in an intriguing personal story—about growing up on a boat, say, or having an influential mentor. If you've been saving a juicy nugget, serve it up now. "Partners actually say to each other afterward, 'Did you talk to the one who told the story about the tidal wave?'" says the former Booz Allen recruiter. "It doesn't matter what they remember you for as long as they remember you."

Body Language: It's Not What You Said

In all likelihood, an interviewer won't browbeat you, torture you, or threaten you with jail time, but that doesn't mean the session won't feel a bit like an interrogation. The room is often cramped and spartan. Every word echoes, every movement is accentuated. It's enough to make a candidate forget about a job and start thinking about an alibi.

In such an environment, an interviewee's body language—how he crosses his legs or sits in the chair—can actually make more of an impression on the interviewer than whatever well-rehearsed words might spill from his lips. Reams of psychological research suggest that while most facial expressions, body postures, and movements don't communicate information per se, they *do* advertise an attitude. And the wrong attitude can mean the difference between a fat signing bonus and "we'll keep your resumé on file."

A Hands-On Attitude

The most vexing question that many interviewees ask themselves isn't "Should I hold out for a company Lexus?"

but rather "What should I do with my hands?" Does folding them on the lap seem controlled or passive? Does gesticulating make someone look energetic or like an irate cabdriver? The answer depends on the interviewer, according to psychologist Laurence Stybel, president of Stybel Peabody & Associates, a Boston-based career management service that prepares senior executives for job interviews. Before deciding what to do with your hands, Stybel suggests that you analyze the language the company uses in its job description. If it tosses around energetic adjectives like *fast* and *rapid*, then sawing the air with your hands sends the right message because it indicates a willingness to be aggressive. If the company prefers *consistency* and *reliability*, place your hands quietly on your lap.

Lip Service

Touching your lips can be an indicator of deception, says Mike Caro, known throughout the high-stakes gambling world as the Mad Genius of Poker. "If a speaker touches or obscures her face, especially her lips, there's a better-than-usual chance that you have just heard something that was uncomfortable to say, and that the speaker may have been lying or exaggerating," explains Caro. And he should know: He makes a living reading the subtle cues of his opponents. Two tips for appearing on the level: Show the palms of your hands during an interview, or touch your chest with your palm.

Armed and Dangerous

Like the word *aloha*, crossing one's arms can communicate many things. Sadly, defensiveness, insecurity, inflexibility, and closed-mindedness aren't going to earn anybody a company trip to the Big Island. "It's almost like you're saying, 'What more do you people want from me?'" says Jody Swartzwelder, former assistant director of campus recruiting for Arthur Andersen in Dallas.

The Handshake

An interviewer's first impression of you is often formed when you shake hands—which is why you should never, ever extend a hand that is even slightly moist. Sweaty palms say one of three things: "I'm out of shape and frightened," "I am vaguely reptilian and therefore wholly untrustworthy," or "I am perhaps just a little bit too happy to meet you."

Angling for Position

Tipping back in the chair is a sure indicator of an interviewee's overconfidence and projects a subtle air of disdain. It's far better, recruiters say, to seem eager than arrogant. But leaning too far forward makes job candidates look as if they might pounce on their interviewers at any moment and demand to know "where the money's hidden." "You want to choose a moderate position that isn't too cocky but definitely lets the interviewer know that you are awake and aware," says Lauren Shapiro, who, as campus manager for Connecticut-based Deloitte Consulting, has supervised more than a thousand interviews.

Legwork

Which makes a stronger statement: legs crossed or feet planted on the floor? "It's hard to get comfortable in an interview, so choose whichever position puts you at ease," says Shapiro. She does caution, however, that if you cross your legs, they should be crossed all the way. "Resting your ankle on your knee conveys an overly casual attitude," she says. The most important thing, though, is to find a position and stick with it. Constant shifting can make an interviewee look, well, shifty.

Don't Touch Your Nose

Studies conducted at Chicago's Smell & Taste Treatment and Research Foundation show that touching the outside of the nose can be a prime indicator of lying. Guilt associated with deceptiveness triggers a rise in blood pressure, which then causes tissues in the nose to stretch and release histamine. The histamine causes itching, which in turn induces scratching. Recruiters may or may not be up on this research, but why find out the hard way?

Nice Gesture

Job candidates should definitely convey enthusiasm for the position they're after. According to Swartzwelder, pressing your fingers together to form a steeple not only shows interest but also suggests assertiveness and determination. Steepling can be overdone, however, especially when accompanied by a malevolent grin and the words "Your petty enterprise is no match for my cruel ambitions."

Eye Contact

Make it. Avoiding eye contact is unnerving for the interviewer and creates the impression that you're hiding something.

Show You Care

If you get past the interview stage, you may have the pleasure of receiving a salary offer. Most candidates are savvy enough not to break into a rendition of "We Are the Champions" at this point. "The natural tendency would be to look away and act indifferent if an offer is more than a person expected," explains Caro. It's the equivalent, he says, of a poker player with a strong hand acting nonchalant when he wants an opponent to bet. If you want to up your own ante, it might be better to take a direct approach. After all, you're up against a pro.

Nail the Recruiting Dinner
(Business School Special)

Caitlin McLaughlin spends a lot of time in restaurants. As director for MBA recruiting at Salomon Smith Barney, much of her job—making presentations about the firm, answering questions, wooing students, being wooed—actually happens within a few feet of a place setting.

She has seen a great swell of candidates handle themselves with aplomb. But she has also seen the ugly side of the recruiting dinner: the student bright enough to be invited to an open-bar reception but demented enough to order the $185 cognac; the guy who was caught trying to change place cards so he'd be seated closer to the company big shot; not to mention countless other missteps, blunders, and screwups. "We all know that the resumé is not perfect information," says McLaughlin, "which is why the dinner is almost reverse recruiting." That is, recruiters already know what their guests look like on paper, so the real test is seeing how well they handle themselves in a social situation.

How hard can it be? The savvy student shows up, pushes around some pasta, waxes eloquent about the Nasdaq, and hits 'em with the charm train so hard their heads hurt. Right?

Well, not exactly. After all, if recruiting dinners were such a cakewalk, the firms wouldn't bother with them. With much at stake and with so many potential pitfalls, it takes a deft combination of tact, assertiveness, and savoir faire to shine in these circumstances. In other words, eat before leaving home, because it's not about the food.

Something to Chew On

Considering that a candidate, if hired, will likely be wining and dining clients, manners are something a recruiter can't help but notice. Everyone knows not to chew with an open mouth, but consider a few less obvious deal breakers that recruiters have noted: mopping up sauce with the bread; cutting an entrée into a lot of bites rather than one bite at a time; eating too quickly. Regardless of what looks enticing on the menu, avoid ordering soup, spaghetti, lobster, ribs—anything that could possibly make you look like a slob. And though recruiters profess not to judge people by their menu choices—for instance, deciding that someone is sheepish because he ordered the salad as an entrée—they do notice the matter of price. "Anything in the extreme draws attention," says Dana Ellis, former director of recruiting for Arthur Andersen. "If everyone's having the $9 cheeseburger, and some guy orders a $35 steak with an $18 appetizer, it looks bad."

On the subject of looking bad, eat what is served, however undercooked, charred, or otherwise unpalatable. "On the whole, fussy is bad," adds Ellis. "If someone's picky about their food, maybe they'll be picky about their job assignments, or who they'll work with, or about having to make a 7 A.M. meeting." If you're a vegetarian and the recruiting dinner is in a steak house? "Well, my heart goes out to you," says Ellis. "But I wouldn't make a big deal about it."

If a waiter happens to serve you the wrong item altogether, or something that's flat-out inedible, bring it to his attention—but do so subtly. Although some candidates evidently think it makes them look like a take-charge type, don't rigorously hail the server; eye contact and a discreet tilt of the head will carry the day. (There are rumors of firms arranging for this to happen to see how a candidate handles mix-ups.) "Err on the side of being too polite to the servers. Even the mildest condescension toward a waiter is a huge negative," says McLaughlin. "One of the things we're looking for is the capacity to deal with people at all levels. When somebody takes a superior attitude, you have to wonder how well they're going to work in a team at our company."

Drink But Don't Be Merry

"A lot of companies will let you have a few drinks to see how you do," says Charles Sacarello of Charles & Associates, a New York–based image-consulting firm that whips boorish spouses of CEOs into shape. "They look for whether you loosen your tie or take off your jacket when no one else has. That sort of thing."

When it comes to alcohol, most recruiters advise following the host's lead before ordering—that is, having a beer or cocktail only if the rep does so first—though abstaining is not necessarily a negative mark. A few other points to re-

member: Cup your hand when squeezing a lime wedge over
a gin and tonic. Drink beer from a glass. When it's time to
head to the dinner table, leave cocktails on the bar. Once
seated, drink what the host drinks with the meal. (This is
not the time to showcase one's individuality, let alone one's
knowledge of rare Lebanese wines.) Refrain from com-
pletely draining the wineglass at any point during the meal.
Refrain from refilling your own glass (let the waiter do
that). And by all means, do refrain from that human-
garbage-pail, bottoms-up move when it's time to go.

A Little Practice

It's an odd contradiction: While the American workforce is
becoming better educated, better traveled, and increasingly
professional, knowledge of basic manners doesn't seem to
be keeping pace.

"I've had a client tell me, 'This person is brilliant and
handsome, but we took him to a restaurant and everything
changed. His tie was over his shoulder, his face was over his
dinner plate, he ordered wine when he shouldn't have,'" says
Sue Fox, author of *Business Etiquette for Dummies* and president of Etiquette Survival, a California-based company that
helps Silicon Valley executives polish their acts. "This was a
guy who was going to be called upon to host the company's
Japanese clients—and they would have been mortified."

Those with a tendency to get spots on their ties or who
feel even slightly uncomfortable dining in business attire

might consider practicing. One way is to eat at home in a jacket for a week. The producers of the original James Bond films are said to have made Sean Connery do as much, and it clearly paid off for him. It's worth rehearsing your manners, too. Although recruiters downplay the formality of their outings as well as their own knowledge of the minutiae of etiquette, the professional manner-meisters claim that future employers look for polish without knowing it. "Companies are trying to find future executives, people who will project the image of the firm," says Sacarello. "Bone up on this stuff ahead of time," adds Fox. "Because you don't want to be distracted by thinking about what glass to use while you're being interviewed. You want to spend that time asking smart questions."

As it happens, recruiters say, they're more likely to schedule meals at noisy, hip places than at morguelike restaurants where a person can hear the silver clink. So candidates can look out of step if they show up dressed for a board meeting. Recruiters agree that if someone is uncertain about what to wear, it's entirely sensible to scout the restaurant beforehand or to call the person organizing the dinner to ask about appropriate dress.

Dining with Sharks

As if social blunders weren't enough to worry about, there are fellow classmates to deal with. Where the cautious student may find himself laboring not to appear either overzealous or underambitious, there's a decent chance that the competition is going to be overtalking, undermining, and outhustling him for the job. B-school lore is rife with stories of job candidates acting to advance their interests at the expense of their classmates: from the student who kept the date of a recruiting reception to herself to the guy who put up fake flyers announcing a change of venue for a dinner.

Perhaps most annoying are those who think nothing of striding into the middle of your three minutes with the recruiter and hijacking the conversation. Should this happen, do not roll your eyes. Do not throw an elbow. Do not get caught up in the petty race for airtime. Stay composed and polite, and remember that if the guy looks obnoxious to you, he'll look obnoxious to the recruiter.

That said, you don't want to squander your few minutes with a recruiter. "Don't go without having three points to make about yourself," says Ronna Lichtenberg, author of *Work Would Be Great If It Weren't for the People*, a lucid guide to office politics. "It might be something you are skilled at or would like to do in a work setting, or an aspect of the company you'd like to know more about. Whatever it is, if you have three positives in the cupboard, you'll feel more in control of the conversation."

And if the feeding frenzy starts to get out of hand? First, resist any urge to make fellow candidates look bad. It's a strategy beyond the skills of most, and one that can backfire badly. "You don't look good by attacking someone," says

Lichtenberg. "If someone comes after you—say, someone tries to make something you said sound dumb—don't defend your comment. Instead, say something like, 'I guess you have a lot more experience with this topic than I do. Why don't you tell me more?' Bullies and braggers don't have a sense of proportion. They'll roll on and on, and hang themselves." And if another student is hogging the floor? "Let them go on all they like as long as you've made your points," she says. "Don't worry about the other student. It's the recruiter who matters."

At most recruiting dinners, the company will send along a variety of representatives from different levels of the organization and rotate them from table to table during the predinner mingling. Avoid the mistake of snubbing the junior-level associate to chum up to the big dog. "Everybody within our firm is equally important—that means the staff setting up the dinner as well as the managing directors," says SSB's McLaughlin. "Don't race past a VP to start schmoozing an MD. We're all there together and everyone's opinion counts when we trade notes afterward." McLaughlin points out another risk inherent in racing up to the chief: "If you sit next to the senior partner but aren't comfortable talking about the highest levels of business, you have more of a chance of blowing it than if you sit next to a junior associate who's recently out of business school." Not to mention that it's far easier for him to picture you in his seat a year down the line.

CHAPTER 5

Tips for Specialty Interviews

WHEN IT COMES TO INTERVIEWING, EVERY INDUSTRY
has its own idiosyncrasies and expectations. The attitudes
and mannerisms a bank wants to see—even when you're answering basic questions like "Why do you want to work for
us?"—could sink you at a start-up. Try telling a buttoned-
down banker that "I love to create new projects and run with
them." You might as well run for the door. Or go ahead and
don a suit and tie for your next interview at a start-up—but
it might be faster if you just wrote the word *Dullard* on your
forehead instead. Here, we offer the dos and don'ts when interviewing at a consulting firm, bank, law firm, and start-up.

Interviewing at a Consulting Firm

You don't have to be Sherlock Holmes to ace the cases in a
consulting firm interview. In fact, a little preparation can

make solving them seem, well, elementary. Remember your seventh-grade algebra teacher's three favorite words? "Show your work." At the time, it seemed silly: Why not just *show the right answer*? Now that you're older and wiser, however, you know that in many cases, how you get to the right answer is more important than simply knowing the answer itself.

The same goes for the case questions that consulting recruiters lob at you. Consulting is a demanding job with few "correct" answers; this method of interviewing gauges how well you manage the process of getting to an answer and how you perform under simulated client-engagement conditions.

We talked to consultant-hunters at several recruiting firms to glean their advice on cracking the case interview. Here's what they revealed—and how you can best prepare.

Why the Case Interview?

Case interviews have long been used by recruiters to observe a candidate's thought processes in motion. Can you deconstruct and analyze complex, open-ended business problems? Do you stay calm, or will you sweat bullets under pressure at a client site?

At the most basic level, a case interview is about asking the right questions, developing a logical way of working through the relevant issues, and arriving at a recommendation. Your structure may be a packaged framework or it may be various frameworks strung together; you may even choose not to use frameworks at all. What's important is that you demonstrate *some* defined structure.

"Case studies are an imperfect science," concedes Michael Gibney, project manager at PricewaterhouseCoopers, "but are easily implementable in the thirty to forty-five minutes we have for each interview." Since they measure your analytical skills, they're an improvement over simple "fit" or "resumé" interviews.

In most case interviews, the recruiter gives you an example of a real-life client problem. Some typical categories include:

- Company Strategy: "My client is thinking of making an acquisition, and . . . "
- Brain Games: "How many tennis balls are in the United States?"
- Operations Improvement: "Why is my client's factory running behind?"
- Market Size: "How big is the global air-conditioner market?"

Although each requires a slightly different approach, all are meant mainly to evaluate the process you use, not the answer you come up with.

Practice Makes Perfect

You absolutely, positively must prepare in advance for case interviews. "It becomes pretty clear pretty fast who has—

and who has not—practiced," says Gibney. "I know there is a basic sort of business acumen that may not be able to be practiced, but candidates must have an understandable approach to solving problems. That's what our clients demand of us. If we can't relate solutions to the client, it's a problem."

If you attended a case-oriented business school, don't assume that will give you an upper hand. John Flato, former Cap Gemini Ernst & Young's national director of university recruiting, says these candidates don't seem to do any better or worse than others.

Study different kinds of case questions. Just because your buddy interviewed before you and gave you a heads-up on the questions doesn't mean you'll get the same ones. Recruiters have tons of case questions in their repertoire, and the chances of their using the same question multiple times on one campus visit are slim to none.

Get a friend to role-play the interview with you, and use any resources (such as a casebook) that your school's consulting club provides. The more mock cases you sink your teeth into, the more likely you are to be relaxed and poised for the real thing. Sometimes you learn more by presenting a case question to someone than you do when solving the case yourself.

Deliberately pick industries you're not familiar with to test your analytical skills, not your ability to memorize; for instance, if your pre-B-school experience is mostly in media and entertainment, get your case buddy to ask you about steel production or medical-device marketing. That said, do consider brushing up on the basics in several industries—for instance, know the product development cycle in pharmaceutical research, and understand current trends in technology. Although each case is different, with practice you will improve your analytical reasoning skills and solution method.

Think Through the Process

When it comes to strategy or product marketing questions, the interviewer will often give you only the bare bones of a case and will wait for you to request further details: How many competitors does the company have? What are the major cost and revenue drivers? Who are the major clients? And don't forget to ask for the firm's mission—if you don't know what a company's goals are, you might come up with a valid but misguided solution.

A sample question Gibney used recently involved a manufacturer/distributor/retailer of computer products. This client has traditionally gone directly to the consumer and has developed a solid brand image. The client now wants an assessment of the issues relating to the core business, as well as the opportunities for the company to get into the services side, which it views as a high-margin, high-growth-rate business. The candidate now needs to provide an approach or evaluative framework for analyzing each of the two different problems.

As long as it's permitted, work your answers out on paper. Pencils and pens, plus a notebook or legal pad, should be standard equipment in any case interview. "It's amazing how many people show up without a pen and paper," says Kamenna Rindova, a former senior associate at Mercer Management Consulting. Thinking through all the facts is a must, and you're not going to do it all in your head.

May the Five Forces (Not) Be with You

Some recruiters are turned off when potential hires draw on a packaged analytical framework (such as Porter's Five Forces) to solve a problem. Others, however, are impressed. To be on the safe side, if you use a framework, don't stray too far from the issue.

Eileen Coveney, vice president at L.E.K. Consulting, warns candidates about the perils of frameworks: "When people depend too much on a preestablished framework, they may not be thinking deeply enough about the problem at hand. This may indicate that when presented with an actual client issue, they are not going to focus on the details and specifics of the client's problem. Rather, they may be inclined to jump into easy and obvious solutions."

If you do use a framework, choose wisely. If the case is about a business that's considering entry into an industry, the Five Forces may indeed be your best bet. If you're talking about how products get from suppliers to end consumers, consider the value chain. Companies that are falling short on sales could use a profitability or cost versus revenue analysis.

"Is That Your Final Answer?"

Don't be afraid of pausing. Take the time to make notes and sketch out the problem. Don't blurt something out unnecessarily to end a period of silence. You're not on a game show. You're interviewing to be a consultant, which is a business as much about thinking as it is about communicating. Above all, be calm.

If you do respond to a question too quickly, before understanding all the facts, you may end up contradicting yourself halfway through your response—which could be disastrous. "In our environment and our industry," says Sean Huurman, national recruiting director of KPMG Consulting, "we need to make sure we're saying the right thing the first time."

After all the analysis, however, don't forget to come to some kind of conclusion as to what the company should do. Consider presenting a decision rule that the imaginary organization could use to figure out what the best option is—e.g., if revenues outstrip costs, then do X.

Follow the Leader

Many firms use a group exercise in their second or subsequent rounds to see how well you work with others. If you're assigned a role other than team leader, don't fret. It doesn't matter what your role is in the exercise—just do it well. If you and the other team members are told to settle among yourselves who gets to do what, don't fight over who gets to make the presentation or lead the group. Likewise, don't play the shrinking violet. Remember, the recruiter is watching.

Whatever you do, show confidence, not arrogance. A display of ego before Flato is a certain red flag. "We hire bright and talented people, but only those who can work well with team members and not display arrogance," Flato says.

Ready for some company-specific advice? Here's what five recruiters told us about interviewing at their firms.

Recruiter No. 1: Eileen Coveney, Vice President, L.E.K. Consulting

The Questions.   Testing a candidate's skill across a range of areas is the primary reason L.E.K. uses case interviews. Coveney indicates that the case interviews are meant to (1) assess a candidate's analytical ability, (2) evaluate a candidate's communication skills and logic flow, (3) understand how a candidate responds to redirection, and (4) test his/her overall fit with the firm. Most questions L.E.K. recruiters ask center on strategic growth opportunities for potential clients.

Words of Wisdom.   Coveney doesn't have a preference regarding how a candidate initially reacts to the case interview question. "Some people take some time to formulate their thoughts, other people ask a few questions, and other people jump right in," Coveney says. "Relax and take your time, focus on the specific issues of the case, remember there is no one right answer to the case, and don't use too many frameworks. Don't throw in the kitchen sink, like Porter's Five Forces, etc. Just be confident, and relax—it will really help with the interview."

Recruiter No. 2: Kamenna Rindova, Former Senior Associate, Mercer Management Consulting

The Questions.   MMC asks most candidates one-on-one questions and doesn't often do group exercises. Reflecting the firm's focus, most questions deal with strategy issues, with occasional market-sizing questions thrown in. The purpose of the interview for MMC is to assess the candidate's ability to structure and think through a problem as she would on the job.

Words of Wisdom.   Rindova says practice and familiarity with cases is essential, and stresses that an interview can go south if the candidate loses sight of the structure he or she is building. Lastly, beating a clear path to any response is more important than getting it right. "You can give (a recruiter) a wrong answer, but if you thought out loud through the process, you could still have a stellar interview," Rindova says.

Recruiter No. 3: Scott Berney, Former Head of U.S. Recruiting Operations, Monitor Group

The Questions.   Determining a person's analytical skills, comfort with manipulating numbers, and ability to integrate different pieces of data is the purpose of the case interview for Monitor Group. For the first round of interviews, case questions are usually written and are two to three pages in length. In the final round, a group event is used.

Words of Wisdom.   "My take on most other firms is that they put a premium on [the candidate's] ability to ask questions in the interview. Monitor cases put a premium on your ability to analyze data, manipulate numbers, integrate, and come up with an answer based on the data you've been given," says Berney. Like L.E.K.'s Coveney, he doesn't like to see candidates use too many frameworks to solve a problem.

Recruiter No. 4: Sean Huurman, National Recruiting Director, KPMG Consulting

The Questions.   "The case question helps get to a thinking process and various characteristics of a candidate you don't necessarily get in an ordinary interview," says Huurman. "When we use cases, we are really focusing on things that tie into the client." The typical KPMG consultant hunter wants to know how a candidate can communicate with the company's team, its leadership, and the client.

Huurman favors group interviews, and he knows a lot of candidates can be prepped in advance but notes that there's "no amount of coaching" that can prepare you for a group project.

Words of Wisdom. "Too many people jump right into the case study and don't put any thought into it," says Huurman. "I want the interviewees to think things through." KPMG recruiters are always told to let the candidate have some time to think through the case, but Huurman indicates that very few candidates take advantage of it.

Huurman admits that few recruiters would ask interviewees what KPMG stands for (curious? It's Klynveld, Peat, Marwick, and Goerdeler), but it's important to do your homework on the firm's services, strengths, and culture.

Recruiter No. 5: Michael Gibney, Project Manager, PricewaterhouseCoopers

The Questions. Some of PwC's competencies don't require that a case question be asked, but it's probably best to plan for one. Interviews are typically one-on-one and are meant to test the business acumen of a candidate. Seeing candidates' insight into business problems and their approach to solving them (most questions are based on true-life client engagements) is the overall goal.

Words of Wisdom. Gibney understands that many problems are too big to solve during the course of a half-hour interview, but he wants to see a firm grasp of key issues. "The candidate must have an understanding of the overall situation and the overall problem, and then create an approach to solve it," Gibney says. "For instance, if we're talking about a client getting into the services business, I would expect to see some kind of framework around identifying what relevant services would be, and the different market and company factors involved. I want the candidate to relate directly what the core issues are."

Interviewing on Wall Street

If consulting firms attract the type A personality, then the world of investment banking attracts type A+. Are you a workhorse? Do you find yield curves sexy? Do you debate the quality of company valuation methods the way sports geeks debate the quality of baseball teams? Great. But the top-tier firms are looking for more than sharky, number-crunching quant jocks: They're looking for passionate team players with the stamina to climb the ladder—from associate to vice president to managing director to . . . Master of the Universe.

Unlike a consulting interview, which lends itself to cool, cerebral case studies and brain games, the investment banking interrogation tends to focus on the personal and the practical. You may be required to do some rigorous intellectual modeling, but don't expect to focus on airy, academic questions. Instead, expect nuts and bolts: "How would you value company X?" "What company would have a higher

P/E ratio, a food company or a pharmaceutical company?" "Where are interest rates going, and why?" "Give me an example of how you manage risk." But never lose sight of the fact that the single biggest question lurking in the background of any I-banking interview is one that is seldom asked directly: "How committed are you to this profession and our company?" It's expensive for an investment bank to train associates, and you won't be giving them value until you're trained. So think commitment—and make your commitment credible.

Know Thyself

You must be in command of your resumé and the story it tells about you. Ideally, you'll be able to talk in detail about any finance experience you have had, or at least projects you've done in business school or elsewhere that are relevant to investment banking. If you're interested in the sales and trading side of the business, remember: Life can be both an ongoing sales pitch and an exercise in risk management. Comb your past for anecdotes that make those points. "If, at sixteen, you convinced your reluctant parents to let you go to a foreign country where you didn't speak the language, I think that tells me a lot about your selling skills—and the way you thrive on a challenge," says a recruiter at Goldman Sachs.

In any case, you must demonstrate that you are a glutton for hard work. "We're looking for people who are into a hundred million things, who need more than twenty-four hours in their day for everything, but are still focused," says Sheila Marmon, a former associate at Morgan Stanley. What to do: Talk about a situation where you (or, better yet, you in a team context) performed well under extreme pressure. If you started a club, led an organization, or ran your own business, make sure you discuss that.

But go easy on the entrepreneurial spirit. A little can go a long way; too much can make you unhirable. "Of course, we want entrepreneurial people," says Carlos Valle, managing director of GMI global recruiting at Merrill Lynch. "But if I see someone was running a business in high school, two businesses in college, and one in B-school, I know they're going to get restless here very soon." If you're an incorrigible entrepreneur—and your resumé will tell the tale if you are—focus on aspects of entrepreneurship relevant to investment banking. When questioned about your experiences, offer something like: "When I was running my business, I needed to produce a model of sales versus expected returns, and here's how I did it." Or try: "Here's how I used the idea of option variation while I was developing a business plan."

Among the many tricky questions you might face, here's a favorite: "Do you have a favorite industry?" You probably do, and you should seize the opportunity to display your passion, but don't create the impression that you'd only be happy working on deals in, say, the software sector. Seldom will you be able to write your own ticket. "We had a guy here who was an MD/MBA who wanted to focus exclusively on health care," says Valle. "He was the very top of the top, and he can do that." A better bet is to be open to the firm's needs and the demands of the market. If you've had great success in high-tech, point it out, but suggest that you could be just as good anywhere else. The same rule applies to ethnic background or cultural interest. If you speak fluent Spanish and have worked well in South America, you've probably got what it takes to be successful in any overseas context.

Know Thy Firms—And Thy Coveted Job

It may sound obvious, but you need to be able to define what investment banking is and explain what an investment banker does in plain language. And you should be attuned to differences in investment banks, both obvious and subtle. Lehman Brothers does a lot of bond deals. Morgan Stanley and Goldman Sachs have retail distribution. Know their tendencies, and their street lore, too. "Goldman has a reputation for being team-oriented; Morgan Stanley was always known for encouraging individuals and mavericks," says Marmon.

Current events are your friends. You can find valuation techniques in books, but you can't teach common sense about—or interest in—day-to-day finance. The latter is what firms are looking for. If Merrill Lynch's P/E is two-tenths lower than Goldman's, you should be able to say why. If the firm is working on a well-publicized deal with company X, you should have an opinion about it before you walk into the interview room. Make sure you're conversant in the recent history of the investment bank, too: major deals, forays into new markets, and so on. If an interviewer lobs a question about a current merger and wants to know what you think, be able to refer to precedents and make specific comparisons with them. You may even have to refer to the very recent past: Some interviewers have been known to ask candidates what the company's stock price was yesterday.

That kind of insight and quick recall is key. The temptation during a job search is to cast your net as wide as possible. But apply to too many firms, and you'll dilute your precious knowledge of each one. "Know the company's literature and their buzzwords, of course," says Merrill Lynch's Valle. "But to do a great interview, you need to contact alumni who work there and find out what the company thinks is critical to its success. You also need to keep up-to-date and fluent on what it's doing, internally and in the business press. You can't really do that with twenty firms."

All of this prepares you for the inevitable questions: What makes us different from our competitors, and why do you want to work here? A good answer will be revealing of both yourself and the firm. For example: "I'm interested in working here because you've focused on market Y and market Z, rather than trying to serve everyone, and your firm encourages individual initiative by . . . "

Quant—The Measure of Some Things

Relax. If you've made it into the interview stage at an investment bank, you can most likely multiply 23 x 17. Your interviewers know this, and they'll be apt to keep most of their quantitative questions practical. "I'm probably not going to ask you to do math in front of me or build some elaborate model," says Raul Gutierrez, a VP at Morgan Stanley. "But I will ask about a current deal we're working on, what kind of accounting issues need to be investigated, and I'll expect you to see that it depends on the industry and to be able to refer to comparable deals in the past."

Still, you do need to know the hows and whys of basic valuation techniques: how to use multiples of sales to evaluate start-ups, or earnings multiples to value an established firm. Refresh your memory of big concepts like the Capital Asset Pricing Model. But remember that such evaluations are as much art as they are science. And don't use jargon carelessly. "If you're truly a finance jock, go ahead and dive into the details," says Marmon. "Just know what you're doing. I remember a job candidate who responded to a question by saying, 'Well, you need to use a P/E ratio.' When we asked him why, it was obvious he didn't know what he was talking about."

If the interviewers want to play brain games ("How many public telephones are there in the United States?"), keep in mind that they're looking for the quality of your thinking process, not the correct answer. The same goes for classic sales-and-trading interview questions like, "Okay, you think you can sell? Sell me this pencil." But you're more likely to be asked a gut-check question that forces you to make a quick choice with limited information. "I once asked a candidate, 'If you were a trader, and with one trade, you had a 50 percent chance of making $100,000, and with another, you had a 20 percent chance of making $1 million, which trade would you choose?' The guy went conservative and explained why. He got the job offer." The lesson: The key part of this is the "why," not the "right" answer. "They're looking for people with strong opinions and convictions," says one trader at Goldman Sachs. "They're less interested in what those convictions are than in how you've arrived at them."

A Strong Finish

When you get a chance to turn the tables and ask questions at the end of the interview, do it wisely. "It can be the most important test you pass," says Neil Rothenberg, a former I-banking associate at UBS Warburg who interviewed countless job candidates. "Ask provocative questions that imply your long-term interest." Some examples:

"Could you describe the corporate culture here, using specific examples?"

"How are decisions made within the organizational hierarchy at this firm?"

"Has there been any recent attrition in management?"

All of these are challenging questions—and all of them suggest you're looking at the big picture. More important, perhaps—in asking them, you're answering that one big question: "Yes, I'm prepared to commit for the long haul."

Interviewing at a Law Firm

First step: Get a law degree. Law firms are notoriously picky about this. Assuming that's taken care of, let's get down to business.

We asked a panel of top legal experts to share with us their favorite interview questions. Then we had real law students give their answers. When you see how perfection-challenged many of the replies were, you'll realize that answering interview questions isn't as easy as it seems (you may also understand why the participants asked not to be named).

Fortunately, our recruiting pros graciously evaluated the students' answers and offered their expert advice on how they—and you—could do better. Here, everything you need to know to impress the best.

What got you interested in the law?

"I've been exposed to the law my whole life. A lot of my
  family members are lawyers."

[New York University student]

"The intellectual stimulation and wanting to help people.
  Also, the reputation."

[Boston University student]

"My parents said I'd make a good lawyer because I like to
  argue and debate. But it wasn't until I was a paralegal—I

worked on real estate transactions and foreclosures—
that I realized I truly liked the profession."

[Rutgers-Camden student]

Bad

Playing the family card ("A lot of family members are
lawyers") or the natural aptitudes card ("I like to argue and
debate") may be logical enough from a student's point of
view, but recruiters hate both tactics. They're overused, and
interviewers are sick of hearing them. Plus, family stories
show "intellectual laziness," says Gail Flesher, chair of the recruiting committee at New York's Davis Polk & Wardwell.
Talking about your parents marks you as juvenile, and "Also,
the reputation" is flat-out off-putting. "Like it appeals to the
girls or the boys in the bar? That wouldn't fly with me," says
Michele Jawin, an executive with Mestel & Company, a recruiting firm in New York and Washington, D.C. In general,
the answers aren't nearly specific enough about each student's unique motivation. To succeed at a law firm, says Kim
Koopersmith, a hiring partner at Akin, Gump, Strauss,
Hauer & Feld in New York, "you have to really want to do
this. It's not an easy way to make a living, so you had better
have thought it through on your own."

Good

The last piece of the Rutgers student's answer establishes the
kind of personal connection that recruiters are looking for,

says Akin, Gump partner and hiring committee member Andrew Rossman. Saying "I was a paralegal [and] I realized I truly liked the profession" may not seem like a home-run answer, but it doesn't have to be. The point is, the student took a firsthand experience and related it to her decision to become a lawyer. "That's real," says Rossman. "That I can accept."

The Bottom Line

Be prepared to talk about a concrete personal experience that led you to the law. If you have something big, great—go with it. JeanMarie Campbell, Akin, Gump's manager of legal recruitment and professional development, recalls one student, for instance, whose parents were killed in an accident; a lawyer helped the student with estate and finance issues, and that inspired her to go into the law. But you don't have to have the slam-dunk reason. Recruiters realize that most law students have had neither much practical legal experience nor a life-altering episode that drew them to the field. Just be sure your reason paints you in a flattering light. Consider the BU student's answer about "intellectual stimulation." "If that's true, that's perfect," says Flesher. "If you worked as a paralegal, great. You have to have a reason, though. There's got to be a reason."

Why do you want to work in a law firm?

"Working in a firm will expose me to many practice areas and different partners and associates."

[NYU student]

"I'll grow and learn the most in a firm environment. I want to learn different areas of law because I feel I'm too young to commit myself to one specialty."

[BU student]

"When I worked for a law firm in Florida, I liked the opportunity to help the client. I also liked when the attorneys brought in novel problems and issues. I realize that a corporate environment would offer the same type of problem-solving opportunities, but a law firm will offer more diversity as to the types of problems and the opportunities to help clients."

[Rutgers-Camden student]

Bad

Me, me, me. You're definitely on the wrong track if your answer implies that a firm should cater to your desires (see "Working in a firm will expose me to many practice areas," and "I'll grow and learn the most in a firm environment"). To an interviewer, this says you're less interested in helping the firm than you are in helping yourself. It may also imply that you're there to get your basic training, then leave. Yes, you need to find out what the firm can do for you, but do it later, after you get an offer. For now, show the interviewer what you can do for the firm. Another problem: "None of these answers says anything about the business," says Flesher. "There's lots about the work that should be interesting to the applicants, and if it's not, they shouldn't be going to a firm." Yet another mistake: the way the Rutgers student mentioned "a corporate environment" out of nowhere. The remark sends a signal that she may be as interested in business as she is in law.

Good

The Rutgers student tried to connect her answer to a real-world experience that had inspired her to work for a firm. The panelists agree, however, that she should have gone deeper, citing specific cases or matters that she worked on.

The Bottom Line

As with the first question, be prepared to answer this one by citing a personal experience—in this case, one that made you want to work at a law firm (as opposed to, say, a DA's office). Also key to acing this query: Show that you understand the complexity and challenges of practicing law at a firm. After all, why would anyone believe you when you say you'd be good at a job if you don't know what the job entails? Vague answers about "many practice areas" and "different partners" only serve to show how little you know. Instead, talk about a case that the firm has worked on recently, say why you found that matter interesting, and spell out how you could see yourself enjoying—and contributing to—that sort of work. Try something like: "The Stumpington case you handled is obviously going to have a major impact on intellectual property law. That sort of matter is something I think I could contribute to, because . . . " No one expects you to be an expert, but don't present yourself as utterly naive, either. Instead of "I'm too young to commit myself to one specialty," at least try something like "I think my skills and interests could be a good match for your litigation department," says Akin, Gump's Rossman.

What drew you specifically to our firm?

"I'm attracted to firms that have a bicoastal presence, because I'm from California. I'm also interested in a firm that does all kinds of work, because I'm unsure about what I want to do right now."

[NYU student]

"I was attracted to your firm because of its great reputation. And it's in the location I want to settle in.

[BU student]

"I want the opportunity to work in New York City and to try different areas of the law before settling down and developing an expertise in one or two areas."

[Rutgers-Camden student]

Bad

A firm with a "bicoastal presence"? One with a "great reputation"? "In New York City?" The students are describing some fifty-odd firms, the panelists point out. "One question

I ask in our evaluations is, "Interest in the firm?" says Rossman. "I have no basis to say that the BU student has a particular interest in my firm."

Good

Sorry, thanks for playing.

The Bottom Line

There's no excuse for not knowing what a given firm has to offer—or not being prepared to say what about the firm appeals to you. These days, firm websites detail everything from practice groups to starting salaries; stories about firms in legal publications are easily accessible on the Internet; and on-line forums like Greedy Associates offer all manner of inside scoops. Gathering even a few tidbits from these sources will show an interviewer that you've done some homework. Better yet, use your networking skills to make contact with a lawyer at the firm and ask her questions. Saying "I spoke to one of your associates the other day, and one of the things I learned was . . . " is an excellent way to show that you care enough about a firm to go the extra mile. Next, says Akin, Gump's Koopersmith, "make a presentation that explains why this firm is what you're looking for. Say 'I like that you have an international practice' or 'I like that you staff the litigation department in a particular way.' With me, that scores points." Another tip: Avoid expressing your interest in one firm by making negative comments about another. Plain and simple, it's unprofessional.

What did you do last summer?

"I just temped to make some extra money. It was pretty administrative, but I learned a lot about hedge funds, because my boss was meeting with investors, trying to get them to invest."

[NYU student]

"I worked for the Suffolk County district attorney's office in Boston, doing legal research. I used creative skills and also skills I learned as a law student. I approached every situation as a search-and-rescue mission and saw myself as a man my supervisors could depend on."

[BU student]

"I was on a study-abroad program in Beijing. Learning about the differences and similarities between our laws and theirs was fascinating. And developing relationships with the students and professors as well as local residents was thrilling."

[Rutgers-Camden student]

Bad

Oh, where to begin? Let's start with, "I just temped"? "That's just dumb," says Flesher. "And lazy." It's not that there's anything wrong with temping, but use the experience to focus on something substantive, she says. The NYU student was headed in a better direction, for example, when she mentioned learning about hedge funds. But her answer would have been far stronger if she had gone deeper into the specifics of what she learned and how that knowledge affected her interest in the law. Give a demerit to the BU student for the phrases "search-and-rescue mission" and "a man my supervisors could depend on." Both remarks cross the line between self-confident and cocky, the panelists say. (In general, simply state the facts about anything you've accomplished and let the interviewer draw his or her own conclusions.) The Rutgers student, our hero to date, whiffed this question badly. Calling a cross-cultural learning experience "fascinating" comes off as glib and unsophisticated, the panelists say. Interviewers don't care whether you liked your coworkers or bosses. Those answers relate to people skills. And as Flesher says, "We're judging your people skills just by talking to you, so focus on substance."

Good

The BU student was smart to bring up his Suffolk County job. You've certainly got a leg up if you spent your summer working in a DA's office or, for that matter, any law-related job (note: do that). The trouble? You guessed it—lack of specifics. Rossman's suggestion: "Say something like 'There was a case that involved kidnapping. There was an interstate jurisdictional issue about whether you could prosecute someone you know who kidnapped a person in Massachusetts and took them to Rhode Island. I researched it and wrote a memo.'" That speaks volumes about a candidate, Rossman says—what she's done, how she explains matters, how involved she got in the work. "Show me that you're thinking."

The Bottom Line

Koopersmith has a tip that applies to the "just temped" answer—and to all answers, in fact. Before you start talking, take a few seconds to organize your response. The "just temped" answer would have been much better, she says, "if the student had paused and started simply with 'I had an opportunity to work in the hedge fund area, and it exposed me to an area of corporate practice I might be interested in.'"

How will law school help you as a lawyer?

"I feel that my law school education will be invaluable regardless of what I do."

[NYU student]

"My student government experience helped me with my people skills, and my clinic experience taught me how to interview and counsel clients. It also taught me that details should not be overlooked."

[BU student]

"My law school education will open doors for me. With a law degree, the possibilities are virtually unlimited as to what avenues I can explore."

[Rutgers-Camden student]

Bad

The NYU student's ship is sinking fast. If by now you don't recognize the gross failings of that answer (vague, impersonal), your boat will likely go down, too. The BU student's answer may appear to be good, but at least part of it is flawed, says Koopersmith. If you have to talk about student government, she says, "it shows you don't have enough substance." Once again, the Rutgers student has accidentally revealed that the law may not really be a main interest. Her comment about law school's opening doors translates as a lack of commitment to legal work, says Mestel & Company's Jawin. "That makes me nervous. I want to hear something definite about wanting to be a lawyer."

Good

The clarity with which the BU student delivered his remarks about his student government and clinic work showed that he had come prepared (that said, be careful that your answers don't sound canned, even if you've given them a dozen times already). And the law clinic work that the BU student refers to is a solid response. To a law firm, almost any hands-on real-world experience you get in law school is a big plus. That said—have we mentioned this before?—the student could have been more substantive and specific.

The Bottom Line

In a way, the "How will law school help you?" query is a trick question. If all you have to talk about is what classes and professors you liked or what you did in student government, you're not going to impress anyone. If you don't have practical experience (we repeat: get some), translate what you've learned in a class into something that shows why you're interested in—or why you'll be good at—working for a law firm. Try something like "I had a class in which we talked about telecom deals that involved big firms. The most interesting case was X. What I learned was Y. That's exactly the kind of work I think I'd like to do." Or talk about a professor in terms of how she got you interested in an area of the law. "For instance, 'I had a contracts professor who wrote a book on gender-neutral contracts,'" says Campbell. A student could use something like that as a way of saying what she herself is interested in. Red flag: If you find that all you and the interviewer are talking about is law school, "start paddling for shore," says Rossman.

What do you do in your spare time?

"Since starting law school, I've spent most of my spare time tutoring middle-school students, going to the gym, and reading for pleasure."

[NYU student]

"I like meeting people outside of law school. It puts life in perspective. I like to read adventure books like *The Per-*

fect Storm. And I like to work out—jogging, tennis, soccer, basketball."

[BU student]

Reading, playing puzzle games like *Myst* or *Riven*, or watching TV, like Discovery Channel's forensic show.

[Rutgers-Camden student]

Bad

Okay, so no one expects law students to live rock star social lives, but honestly, this is just ugly. Television? Never mention it, ever, no matter how "educational" the shows you claim to watch. Computer games? Never ever *ever* mention them. Leave aside issues of extreme geekdom. "It says that you're a couch potato," says Jawin. Meeting people outside of law school? God help you if you don't.

Good

Tutoring is an honorable way to spend a few hours of your week. Law firms aren't looking for Mother Teresas, but firms do respect people with an altruistic spirit (that said, don't act like you're "above" law firm work). An interest in an activity like tutoring also indicates that "you can focus on something other than yourself and that you use your time constructively," says Koopersmith—and those are traits a law firm definitely values. Of course, we'd be remiss if we didn't point out that the NYU student could have turned her B answer into an A by using . . . yes, specifics. Says Rossman: "She could have tried something like 'I've enjoyed tutoring middle-school students, and for the last year, I've tutored a third-grader, and it's been terrific to watch her development in math.'"

The Bottom Line

You don't have to be healing the sick, winning IQ competitions, or playing on the LPGA tour (though none of that would hurt). Interviewers simply want to see that you have something positive that you're passionate about—something that makes you *you*. The NYU student's answer was perfectly good; a picture of her personality emerges—someone who can focus outside herself. Fine. Finally, here's something to ease your mind: Flesher says she asks this question in part just to see how articulate people are. "I just want to know that somebody can hold an intelligent conversation. It tells me they're skilled in verbal interaction." In other words, it's a lob—sit back, relax, and show off your intelligent, verbal self.

Interviewing at a Start-Up

You're a hardy soul. You eat market downturns for breakfast. The safe move? That's for the other guy. You want a job at a start-up. Of course, interviewing at a fledgling enterprise isn't like strolling in to meet the recruiting manager at a bank or consulting firm. To begin with, you're dealing with the company founders—hard-charging, ambitious types who may not have much organizational experience and who've probably read one too many issues of *Fast Company*. As they see it, their business ideas are their babies— and you're going to be the baby-sitter. Here's how to convince them you're up to the job.

Do the Research

Learning about a company, its leaders, and the industry is essential before any job interview. But with a start-up, where it's not always easy to get the info you need, a little ingenuity can pay off. For instance, one candidate at Square-Trade, an on-line mediation firm in San Francisco, phoned one of the founders and pretended to pitch consulting services. "He asked about the technology, the staff, the equipment," says a former employee. "It helped him know what he was getting into, and he sounded very smart during the interview." In short, be able to show that you're up to speed—or that you can get up to speed in a hurry. It's a huge asset at a new company.

Be a Believer

Employee devotion can mean the difference between success and failure in a company's early days. Founders know this. You, therefore, must get religion. That coy, take-it-or-leave-it act just doesn't play. "I was looking for people who loved the business idea and were not simply looking for a job," says Amy Schrier, founder and CEO of New York–based Blue Media Ventures, which publishes the adventure-travel magazine *Blue*. In 1997, Schrier interviewed a woman whose enthusiasm and thorough research won her an offer. "She was pitching my idea to me," says Schrier. "Her early faith in *Blue* gave me great confidence." The woman is now the company's COO. Do parents ever tire of hearing how cute their baby is? No. And so it is with founders, who, whether they want to admit it or not, love to hear their business strategies validated. One possible line: "A lot of start-ups in your industry have been looking shaky lately, but I think yours is different. Here's why . . . "

Get Ready for Anything

Most entrepreneurs fancy themselves to be maverick types who refuse to play by the establishment's petty rules, so when it comes to interviewing, the process isn't necessarily going to be straightforward. A job offer could come after a single thirty-minute interview or several agonizing rounds peppered with oddball questions like "Who was your favorite *Brady Bunch* kid—and why?" It's also not uncommon to have ten or twelve employees sit in on interviews—with everyone wielding veto power. One well-known founder likes to chat with prospectives as he drives them around in his Porsche. Idealab! founder Bill Gross is famous for scheduling eight- to ten-minute interviews at arbitrary times, like 2:42. The interviewee gets one question, "then Gross talks about the business and judges your reaction until time's up," says one former employee. The winning strategy? Play along no matter what comes your way. Working at a start-up involves dealing with all kinds of unexpected problems; going with the flow shows you can handle it.

Send the Right Signals

Since you'll likely be interviewing with the founders—as opposed to a hierarchy of HR types—you won't get a second chance to make the right impression. The words you may casually toss off can make a big difference. Says Chris Denniston, a cofounder of software maker Agile Systems: "I like it when people use words like *build, adapt,* and *grow,* because that suggests wanting to be part of a team." Other trigger phrases—*making more with less* and *strategic alliances*—suggest a creative, cost-conscious attitude that appeals to founders. On the other hand, says Tony Levitan, cofounder of Shhh Studios, a start-up entertainment company, "avoid asking about 'my assistant' or 'new office space.'" You want to come off as low-maintenance, because you'll probably be changing your own lightbulbs. "Make it clear that you have the initiative to step into the situation and make it happen," says Schrier, "because at a start-up, you'll be working without a road map."

Put Yourself in Play

"If someone demonstrates that she can rally a team to solve a problem, that's a huge plus," says Payton Stiewe, a former hiring manager for the invitation service Evite.com. When offering advice about the company, there's a fine line between insightful and arrogant. "Please don't tell me, 'You need to do this and you need to do that,'" says one Silicon Alley founder—particularly if you haven't been asked. And if you are asked, have ideas ready. Saying "You know more about this than I do, but given the demographics, L.A. looks like a good market" shows both smarts and deference. If it's already in the business plan, say "Great minds think alike," and move on to the next idea.

Dress the Part

"We almost didn't hire a VP of personnel because on his third interview, he was still wearing a tie," remembers Shhh Studio's Levitan about a candidate at a previous company. Business casual is perfectly acceptable at almost any start-up interview. A fashionable button-down shirt, a pressed pair of trousers, and a belt is a solid look for men. (To stand out from the crowd, shine your shoes and don't wear khakis.) For women, a stylish white blouse, a cardigan, and casual slacks will do the trick. Beyond dress, skip the formal salutations and stick to first names. "Don't call me 'Mister' unless you want me to send you on to my dad," says David

Hammond, cofounder of PeopleBonus.com, an on-line job board.

Follow Up—Fast

Skip the fancy stationery. "Send us an e-mail. A short, smart note that furthers a point made in the interview," says Jamie Weissenborn, a former VP of sales and distribution at the now defunct Comedy World Radio Network. "I've sent e-mails from my BlackBerry five minutes after I left the building. You can't follow up fast enough."

Spinning Your Career Switch

LOOKING TO CHANGE CAREERS BUT NOT SURE HOW TO

go about it? One thing that can help grease the skids is an MBA. Some 75 percent of B-school students seek their degrees as the first step in a journey from one field to another. And more often than not, that new field is consulting, banking, or marketing. But whether or not you choose to get a business degree, the right approach to a new field can make a world of difference.

Even in the best of times, employers are more inclined to look within their own industries for viable candidates. And when the job market's tight, it's even tougher for those without direct industry experience. To compete, career switchers need to think strategically. They need to position themselves exactly right. They need, among other things, to highlight the key similarities between their previous jobs and the ones they're gunning for. This goes for resumés, cover letters, and especially interviews.

Our guide to spinning the career switch—compiled with the help of recruiters, placement advisers, and successful switchers—not only tells you what qualities interviewers in various industries are seeking but also gives you tactics to sell them precisely what they're shopping for, regardless of your background.

After all, isn't that what business is all about?

Moving into Banking

Banking is the realm of the vigilant and the acute. You need a thorough familiarity with balance sheets, spreadsheets, and income statements, and, says Ken Gesund, senior recruiter for Merrill Lynch, you must be able to back your recommendations with bulletproof quantitative analysis. Recruiters also want to know that something besides the healthy paycheck is drawing you to the job. Finally, be aware that this is a profession steeped in tradition—rebels need not apply.

Start-Up ⇒ Banking

Anyone coming from a start-up risks being seen as a renegade, someone who has worked in an unstructured environment and, instead of mastering a discipline, has skimmed the surface of everything from financial analysis to brand management to foosball to God-knows-what. That is but one stereotype you need to fight against. "You've got to convince me of two things," says Alison Trumbower, the head of investment-banking-associate recruiting for J.P. Morgan Chase. "That you understand the differences between the environments of a start-up and an investment bank, and that you're not just making this switch because your IPO went sour." In short, she says, "denigrate the start-up stereotypes without denigrating your start-up."

Of course, you've also got to stress the commonalities, such as the immense energy required, and even the specific types of work you did. Did you calculate whether it was better to hire a designer or use freelancers? Whether to buy or lease the copier? That's exactly the type of thinking you'll be doing at a bank, so emphasize it. "Talk about initiative and leadership, but bookend it with how well you work with teams," suggests Trumbower. Letting your interviewer know that you have no problem following orders can't hurt. Also, mention the names of the bank's senior people in a way that demonstrates your respect for structure and superiors.

Marketing ⇒ Banking

You designed an award-winning logo? You wrote the jingle that led the ad campaign? Nobody cares. Here's what's relevant: As a brand manager, you made your case with numbers. You conducted valuation analyses for every potential market and product variety, then persuaded the CEO to give you the money for the launch. "Make it clear that you are not only good at but also passionate about your number-crunching skills," says Al Cotrone, director of the Office of Career Development at the University of Michigan Business School. Stress the variety of product fields you had to run numbers on. And since deals may require twenty-four-hour attention, be sure to mention the nights you spent on the conference room couch before the big launch.

Engineering ⇒ Banking

"Bankers are hesitant to look at people from a technical background, because there's the sense that they're not good communicators," says Monika Drake, a senior associate director at the career management center at Emory University's Goizueta Business School. Your goal? Prove you're the glaring exception. Did you repair a software glitch that opened the lines of communication between production and sales? Skip the technical hoo-ha and talk about how you identified and fixed the problem while winning the cooperation of two competing divisions of the firm. "Describe the analytical measures your fix required and how it cut costs and added value," suggests Jackie Wilbur, director of career development at MIT Sloan.

It's also worth noting that banks hunt for energetic social animals and fierce competitors; the less solitary your hobbies, the better. "If you're a triathlete who hates losing, let them know it," says Drake. "I mentioned I liked the technical part of my previous job, but I didn't like working by myself," says Craig Horstmann, a former project engineer for

Procter & Gamble. "I also told the recruiter I disliked being an overhead expense at the company, where all I did was spend money rather than make it." Today, Horstmann is an associate at A.G. Edwards.

Management ⇒ Banking

"Most general managers haven't been exposed to the long hours and sheer intensity that banking demands," warns a recruiter at a major investment bank. Make it clear that you're prepared for the grueling lifestyle by bringing up the year you attended school full-time and worked the night shift. And while overseeing a production process may seem irrelevant, one recruiter suggests spinning it to your advantage by talking up your ability to quantitatively determine the strong and weak points of the process. That's a skill I-bankers value. Finally, if you worked for a small company and rubbed shoulders with the CEO, mention it; it shows an ability to deal with power players, who are plentiful in banking.

Moving into Consulting

Consultants, the parachute troops of the modern economy, are asked to root out problems like detectives, see the big picture like seasoned insiders, flaunt social skills like party hosts, and flex financial muscle like CFOs. Above all, they are asked for a supreme level of commitment. Says a veteran of a large tech-consulting firm, "Most consulting firms pay a premium because they want to be able to call you on Sunday and say,

'Be on the 6 A.M. to Toledo.'" To secure a job offer, you've got to demonstrate that you're ready, willing, and able.

Start-Up ⇨ Consulting

In the eyes of the consulting recruiter, what you've gained in breadth from helping launch the Good Ship Start-Up, you've lost in depth. As Dana Ellis, former global director of recruiting at Arthur Andersen, puts it, "We want to see not only that you're well rounded but also that you can quickly become a master of one particular area." Job one: Talk up the aspects of the business you concentrated on. Any expertise you have with reorganizing the business plan or deciding to kill off an unprofitable side of the company will be of particular interest to strategy consultants, because they frequently need to size up a company and provide exactly that kind of specific advice for the client.

Another thing firms want to see is that you're able to handle the unexpected—and as you're coming from a start-up, that shouldn't be a tough sell. "Recruiters also want to know that you're a learner," says an MBA from NYU Stern who jumped to consulting. "Risk and experimentation are rewarded in consulting. So don't be afraid to say you failed—as long as you can say you learned, too."

Engineering ⇨ Consulting

Consultants work on a project basis, and, well, so did you. "You'd be smart to stress that you were continuously starting new projects, that you worked on lots of long and short projects that needed to be strung together, all while managing people," says John C. Scott, who switched careers when he went from Nabisco to Andersen. Skip the technical specifics of the revolutionary new packaging you designed for the laser printer and focus on the fact that it was cheaper to make, got more products on the shelf, and was 18 percent more appealing to the customer. "If you're able to describe your experience in a way that elevates the discussion to the larger business problems you were addressing, you'll greatly improve your chances," says Paul Raab, a former executive with A.T. Kearney. Also, mentioning that you regularly met with clients suggests you have the kind of social affability and leadership that's often thought to be lacking in engineers.

Marketing ⇨ Consulting

"In marketing, you're pitching internally, always trying to get funding," says Stacey Rudnick, an MBA from Goizueta who made the switch from a consumer-packaged-goods firm to consulting. "That's not the same as standing in front of a client you've never met and acting like you know more about his industry than he does." That requires thinking on your feet and making your case with irrefutable figures and sparkling insights you've collected from all levels of the production chain. Guess what? Those are precisely the aspects of your job you need to play up. Say you shepherded the market research for a new fashion line. When you talk about it, focus on the managerial component. "Tell them you had to coordinate the 'work streams' of six different teams," says Rudnick. "Consultants love to use the term *work streams*." Tout your proficiency with Microsoft Project, a tool commonly used to manage consulting assignments. And don't forget to let 'em know how much you like to travel.

Moving into Marketing

Whereas bankers dress to display power and consultants dress to fit the client, marketers need to look like they just flew in from Milan. That's because marketing requires a visionary sense, a personal style to match the panache you'll lend to new product lines. And yet behind all that vision and flair, you've got to have the numbers to back up your decisions. "You have to be someone who is comfortable with numbers—analyzing numbers, speaking with numbers, presenting numbers," says Ellen Gilbert, director of recruitment marketing for Johnson & Johnson. Marketers also have to play well with others. "You'll need to look for input from finance, sales, market research, and product-supply departments. The challenge is going to be to leverage the opinions of everyone," says Camille Pierce, senior recruiting manager for Procter & Gamble.

Start-Up ⇒ Marketing

There's no shortage of start-up skills that transfer to marketing, says P&G's Pierce. You can, for instance, focus on the leadership it took to build value from an idea—that is, how you were able to enlist and inspire others to help your company realize a vision. "That kind of risk taking is a great fit," she explains. "You had no guarantees, but you said, 'With this information I have right now, I'm determined to make it work.' We like that." A business plan—with its executive summary, market overview, and cost analysis—is in many ways similar to a marketing plan. Describe the statistical research you did that revealed a new niche. And even if you're leaving BigFlop.com, you can still make some hay. "New marketing initiatives fail in test markets all the time," says Pierce. "Explain your process to the recruiter—why you did what you did in a particular situation and why you decided to pull out." If a brand manager opts not to launch, citing data, he's seen as having saved the company money.

Banking ⇒ Marketing

Among the marketing crowd, finance types are generally thought to be soulless drones planted in front of adding machines. What marketers want is someone with a deep passion for the product itself. Being able to value a company or stock is an important skill, but you must demonstrate that you can then make sense of the numbers with respect to a brand's future, says Maureen Teague, division HR manager at Heinz North America. Talk to your interviewer about why you think specific brands stand out. Then talk about what qualities make their products successful, and suggest ways to implement the same attributes in other products or tactics for selling them to a larger audience. One smart strategy is to compare your previous bank's services with those of its competitors—that is, talk about your bank as a brand—then segue into where you'd like to take the prospective employer's product lines. In short: Be passionate; dress with flair.

Engineering ⇨ Marketing

First and foremost, you need to demonstrate that you have a wide range of skills rather than just mile-deep technical know-how. "If as an engineer you had to make a recommendation as to who was the best supplier or what was the best packing material to use, present that scenario in terms of the skill the decision required rather than the product itself," says P&G's Pierce. Recruiters also want to know that you can look at a problem holistically. "In marketing, quite often all you have is data saying that your share in a consumer segment is down, and you need to determine what the drivers are, put together a plan, and implement it," explains Pierce. Beyond emphasizing that you see the whole picture, it's crucial to play against the engineering stereotype. Do that by underscoring your ability to work with all kinds of people . . . and by not using the word *server* more than once.

CHAPTER 7

Handling Headhunters

A GOOD HEADHUNTER CAN HELP YOU IDENTIFY A NEW
opportunity and install yourself in a new office (and maybe a new tax bracket) in a matter of months. But while most search firms will work hard and honestly for you, lazy and unscrupulous headhunters are far from rare. Some of them overpromise, while others make huge mistakes—like sending your resumé to the firm you currently work for. (Oops.) Here's the cautionary tale of a young Wall Street banker who put his faith in the wrong headhunters. In the section that follows, we'll tell you how to avoid such a colossal waste of your valuable time.

Banking on the Wrong Headhunters

I was laid off from a top-tier investment bank during the Great Banking Purge of 2001. As I started searching for a new job I did what everyone does—I put a lot of feelers out. Maybe that's why a recruiter from a search firm called me saying he had heard of me from a friend at my former employer. The recruiter had some good news, which I needed to hear. He said there was a position open at another top bank, to be an associate in the high-yield investment group.

The job sounded great. As the headhunter put it, this firm was looking for someone more junior than senior, which fit my profile. The details of the job description also meshed well with the experience I had. Perfect. I had been out of work for three months, and things were looking very promising.

The headhunter asked me to come to his office. Before going, I didn't bother to try to check out the firm's reputation. It was a big firm with an impressive address in New York City, so I figured it was legit. I met with three different guys. I gave them my resumé. They were all gung ho about the position and said they were going to send off my resumé right away. They also told me to be ready at a moment's notice to interview for the job and start immediately. "Absolutely," I told them. "Just give me the word, and I'll be there."

I left their offices and went to lunch to celebrate the new job I was pretty sure I'd get. Only minutes after leaving them, I was reading the *Wall Street Journal* when my cell phone rang. It was one of the guys I had just met. Wow. They move fast. But as the guy explained why he was calling, I couldn't believe it. He thought I was someone named

David and was pitching the same job that had been virtually promised to me. "How do you feel about doing high-yield, David?" he asked. Then and there I knew how I felt about this firm—sleazy and, worse yet, incompetent.

I told him who I was and that we had just met and discussed the position not even a half hour before. There was a pause before he made things even worse by saying he did not remember meeting me *at all*. I conveyed my anger, knowing that I would never speak to these guys again.

There's a postscript: During the cell phone conversation, he let slip the name of the firm that was looking for this junior associate. I called the investment bank the next day and wrangled an interview for the very job that had been touted by these jokers. But I didn't get it.

The moral here is as old as business itself—beware the hype. Headhunters will talk a great game and convince you that they are the easiest avenue to finding a job. Don't buy it without thorough examination. All told, I sat across the table from fourteen different headhunters, and they all made big promises, but it was all a waste of time. I didn't get a single interview through them. But I did land a job using my own network. I got in touch with my old boss from my first job on the street, and eventually I joined him at his new firm.

Tips for Happy Hunting

Our banker won't be talking to any headhunters again anytime soon, but you might. And for good reason. It's hard to resist the temptation of a promising job lead, no matter where it comes from, particularly when you're out of work. But to avoid the hassles many people experience with some search firms, we've got one suggestion: Screen a headhunter like you would your daughter's first boyfriend. Run 'em through the ringer. Make 'em earn every bit of information you give them. You'll save yourself a lot of time in the end. The windbags with nothing to offer will get the message and leave you alone. And you'll know that those who survive your due diligence are the real professionals worth your time.

First Things First.   Whether you call a headhunter or she calls you, ask to see her resumé, client list, and six-month placement record before you begin working together. If she's placed people in the types of jobs you desire, that's a good omen for you. While you're at it, get a reference or two. Another important question: If the headhunter found you, ask her how she did it. If you conclude that she found your name on something as random as a sign-up sheet from an event you attended—and this does happen—that suggests the headhunter isn't very selective in how she goes about making matches. Strike one.

The Match Game.   A good headhunter will ask questions about your background and experience before pitching you a specific position. That's the only way for her to find out if you're indeed "perfect for the job." If the headhunter pitches first, consider ditching her.

Meet and Greet.   If the recruiter impresses you on the phone, ask to meet her in person, says Melissa Kahn, a recruiter with an international financial consulting firm. "A lot of the relationship [between the candidate and recruiter] is intuitive, and you can get a feel for the people and how they work by their environment." If the office is a madhouse, chances are you won't get optimal results. And dress for the initial meeting with a recruiter as if it were a job interview, adds Kahn. "Keep in mind that this recruiter is going to be representing you to the company, so you'll want to make her feel at ease about you."

Money Matters.   When talking turkey, provide accurate information about your compensation. You have nothing to lose: The headhunter's fee is based on the salary package you receive, so it's in her best interest to get you the highest salary possible. Fibbing can also come back to haunt you. Most employers ask for your salary history, and lying constitutes grounds for immediate dismissal. Says Debra Grauss, who heads Grauss & Co., an independent recruiting firm focused on financial services: "Why go through the trouble of landing a new position and then destroy all you've worked for with false information?"

Know the Company.   After the headhunter tells you about a position at a company, ask her what she knows about the culture. If the headhunter spouts empty rhetoric—"They're all A-team players"—you'll know she's not very experienced.

Also, ask to see the job description before you indicate interest. Then, if you like what you see, send your resumé with a warm but noncommittal note thanking the headhunter for making you aware of the opportunity.

Be Patient, but Not *Too* Patient.   Until a company asks a headhunter to set up a meeting, she simply might not have anything to report. While there's no industry standard, don't expect to get calls more than once a week. That said, if your recruiter doesn't check in every ten days or so, ask why. Every so often, ask for a "send" list of firms your resumé has been sent to.

Don't Delay.   If you do become a candidate for a recruited position, be prepared to move fast and make decisions quickly. Search firms are usually under pressure from their clients to find someone yesterday, and if you can't keep up, they may pass you over.

Get Real.   If you're a passive job-seeker (e.g., happy in your current job and not necessarily looking to leave), headhunters are happy to have you in their databases. But don't get into an interviewing situation unless you're serious about the opportunity. It's a waste of the search firm's time and the company's time—and the headhunter may not call you again.

Behave Yourself.   There are other misdeeds that could turn a headhunter sour on you: receiving job information from a recruiter, then cutting her out of the loop; getting a job and neglecting to tell her; and being successfully placed by the recruiter, then opting for a job with another company without notifying the first firm of your decision. If you like your new job, touch base with the recruiter and let her know. And recommend the recruiter to others. You never know when you'll need her again.

Feedback Loop. If you get an interview through a headhunter, talk with her beforehand. She should be able to coach you on some of the job responsibilities that will come up during the interview and advise you on how you might anticipate and field questions. And make sure to call the recruiter afterward. Tell her what you liked and disliked about the meeting, because a headhunter may be able to help you negotiate a job offer.

Ditch a Dud. If you're not happy with the work, don't hesitate to call it quits. Request a final send list and ask your recruiter to inform you of any ongoing interview negotiations. Then write her a polite letter stating that you'd like her to end the search and bring all negotiations to a conclusion. Tell her she is no longer authorized to represent you, nor should she put your name in play at any other firms. Says industry veteran Kahn, "You may get a grilling by the spurned recruiter; do not give out any details or indications on where your job search might lead, lest an unscrupulous headhunter pepper you with future calls."

CHAPTER

8

Negotiating the Deal

YOU'VE SWEATED THE JOB INTERVIEWS, SENT THE

thank-you notes, and after a few anxious days of waiting, it arrives—the offer. Sweet. You even high-five the FedEx guy who delivers it. Finally, the nerve-rattling process is over, right? Well, sort of. You might say now is when the real fun begins. Having an offer in hand represents a subtle but important shift in power away from the company and toward you. You're no longer one among many well-heeled candidates angling for the same slot. You're The One. The one they picked over everyone else. The Top Dog. So resist the temptation to immediately say, "Of course I accept. Thank-you sooooo much. I'm so happy, I'll even sweep the lobby on Friday nights." Your first move should be a calm, cool investigation of the finer points of the offer.

Then prepare for the final assent—negotiations.

Dissect the Job Offer

You've heard about the salary and vacation policy. Oh, yeah, the gym membership rocks, too. But trust us, you're probably still in the dark about matters that could determine whether you actually like your new job. How much do you really know about your new boss? Is your guaranteed bonus really guaranteed? Will you have to feed the goldfish every day? Below, we provide a checklist of areas of inquiry so you don't run into any unpleasant surprises after you've already signed on the dotted line.

Does the Offer Have Legs? An offer's only worth as much as the company behind it. "We have a lot of people who don't research the company and don't realize it is in trouble," says Eileen Levitt, president of The HR Team Inc., which provides human resources services for small and midsize companies. "Find out whether the company knows how to make money and not just revenue."

Meet Your New Supervisor. If you didn't interview with your boss-to-be, ask to meet him or her. "You want to know you can work well with that person, to see if the chemistry is there," says Jana Rich, managing director in the San Francisco office of recruitment firm Russell Reynolds Associates. "Ask about management style: What types of people work best with them? How do they evaluate performance?" If you have concerns about your future supervisor, talk to the recruiter about it. But such a conversation should be handled "very gingerly," cautions Sherrie Taguchi, former director of the MBA career management center at the Stanford Graduate School of Business.

Everyday Stuff.   Sure, you know generally what will be expected of you, but make sure you clearly understand the job's little day-to-day responsibilities, too. Sometimes it's those smaller, mundane tasks ("I'll need a daily progress report in writing on every member of the sales force from you") that can make your new gig a grind. And what about the hours? Is this the kind of place where if you leave work before your boss, you'll get a menacing glare the next day? You'll probably hear about the number of sick and vacation days, but you might have to ask about how and when they accrue.

Give and Take.   A signing bonus is a nice thing, but, increasingly, a thing you shouldn't expect. "In 2001, there were a lot of these bonuses," says Dave Opton, CEO and founder of ExecuNet, a Connecticut-based career management services firm that studies trends in executive compensation. "But in the year since, they have dropped from 51 percent of the time to 43 percent." Even if you get one, you could lose it: Some companies require you to pay it back if you jump ship within a certain period of time. So you'd better ask about this—or face having to pawn that spanking-new Cartier watch.

The Disappearing Bonus Trick. Companies love to manipulate performance-based bonus plans. You'll hear that the year-end bonus is more or less guaranteed, only to find out that it can be canceled at management's whim. "Yeah, they are down, too," says Opton. Ask how many times the firm has reduced or killed bonuses in recent years. Calculating bonuses can also be a tricky affair. You may be a top performer and used to getting a full bonus, but some companies also factor in team performance and company profitability. If you're going to be dragged down or lifted up by others, it's nice to know in advance.

Money's Not the Only Option. Stock options no longer hold the allure they did in the late 1990s, and the percentage of cash in compensation packages has risen since then. But because firms continue to hand out options, it's still a good idea to research their value, check analyst reports, and inquire about the vesting timetable. If you have to wait four years to be fully vested, ask yourself whether you expect to stay with the company that long. If you do, options could pay off down the road. "I don't think anyone would ever turn down a stock package as a percentage of the compensation if it's small with long-term value," says Rich.

Healthy Benefits. Because health care has become such a bureaucratic thicket, ask about the problems that tend to arise with coverage and treatment under the company's plan. If you have particular health care needs, find out if the plan covers them. Ask whether you have a choice of managed care or an indemnity plan and how much the premium is for you (and any dependents). Some companies offer a flexible spending account, which allows you to pay medical expenses with pretax dollars.

Feathering the Nest.　Lots of firms have 401(k) plans, but that's where the similarities end. You'll want to know if the company will match part of your contribution—many don't—as well as how long it takes to become vested. As the Enron debacle showed, it also pays to find out if you'll be required to invest in your own company.

Moving On.　If you have a lot of stuff—and you have more than you think—moving expenses can run into the tens of thousands of dollars. Ask for a detailed breakdown of what the company will cover and what it won't. Typical expenses include temporary housing for thirty to ninety days; transporting your household goods (which includes your car); relocation help, such as a house-hunting trip; and a cost-of-living adjustment.

Trial Run.　Taguchi recommends attending a company event, such as a happy hour, to gain some insight into the workplace culture before accepting an offer. You might want to know if company gatherings are, for instance, held on yoga mats with everyone in the downward dog position.

Back to School.   It's not a sexy perk, but for some it can be one of the most important. We're talking about professional development. Adding a new skill to your repertoire may be just the thing to fend off a pink slip down the road. Some companies will pick up part or all of the tab. And by asking about this, you'll appear to be just the kind of motivated go-getter that companies are always looking for.

Toys of the Job.   Even though not everyone needs a company cell phone, everyone wants one. Same goes for a laptop. If the position involves travel or off-site tasks, asking about gadgets is reasonable, says Rich. Otherwise, skip it.

The Give-and-Take

You know the details of the offer inside and out. Now you can confidently enter the final stage of the search process—negotiations. Some job-seekers are too reserved, or grateful, to start haggling. But even if the offer is sweet and the job fantastic, a little back and forth has its place. Some firms want to see you in action and will think less of you if you don't tug a bit. Beyond that, if the offer is full of drawbacks and annoyances, then negotiating it is a no-brainer, because you have little to lose. Be mindful, however, that job negotiations need to be handled delicately so that you send the right message to your new employer—that you're smart, flexible, and only a tiny bit annoying.

Economy Isn't Everything. Generally, a hot economy will expand the range of areas of negotiation, and a cold one will narrow them. But no matter the state of the economy, there's usually room to dicker. Remember, they want you, and they want to make you happy. Although base pay may not always be flexible, companies may be more willing to tweak your start date, office rotation, location, moving expenses, bonus plans, and many other items—even when times are tough. "Most things are open to negotiation," says Stanford's Taguchi.

What? No Negotiations? Businesses that pride themselves on taking big risks will often expect you to negotiate. "I've seen that in hedge funds," says G. Richard Shell, professor of legal studies and management at Wharton and author of *Bargaining for Advantage.* "Firms that make their living on speculation arbitrage and negotiation sometimes make offers to test their employees, to see whether the employee can negotiate. They offer you terms they expect you to improve, and that's what they expect you to do when you get there."

Get with the Program. There are other firms that wouldn't alter their time-tested package for all the charm in the world. Try to find someone in the organization to give you a sense of the firm's position on negotiating. (Don't forget your school's alumni network for access to friendly insiders.) You'll also get a sense of the firm's culture in the interview process—the less formal the company's repre-

sentatives, the less rigid the company is likely to be in negotiations.

Never Negotiate Without an Offer. This is called negotiating
yourself out of a job. Wait for an offer, preferably in writing,
before talking about your compensation expectations and
the like. It shows bad judgment and can be an on-the-spot
deal killer. "That's probably the worst mistake you can
make," says Pri Shah, an associate professor of strategic
management at the University of Minnesota's Carlson
School, who researches negotiation issues.

Patience, Patience. Don't negotiate at the time you receive
the offer. You'll look too impulsive. But call or write immediately, conveying your appreciation and excitement about
the prospect of working for the company.

How Long Can You Think It Over? "I would say a couple of weeks
is fine," says the director of campus recruiting for a global
management consulting firm. "In the offer letter we would
say, 'We look forward to hearing back from you no later
than X.' It's much better if candidates come to us well before
that deadline if they want to negotiate. If they wait till the
last minute, it tells us they're probably shopping our offer."

What Are You Worth? To find out if it makes sense to try to
bump up the salary offer, determine the mean for your position, industry, and region of the country (Salary.com is

one place to look for information about average salaries for a wide variety of industries and positions). "Be ready to tell them where you got the numbers from," says Shah, "so they don't think you got them out of thin air. If you have any information about the terms and perks competitors offer, be ready to mention those. They would appreciate getting the information, too, since they have no way of acquiring that knowledge except through the recruits."

Plan Your Approach.   Before you start the give-and-take routine, make a list of items in the offer you want the firm to improve upon. Be reasonable, because you'll have to justify why it's also in the company's interest to accommodate you. "We take it more seriously when you prepare first," says the recruiting director. "Not everything is negotiable. If you show that you ranked your top three items in order of importance, it shows thoughtfulness and preparation, and those are attributes that we will appreciate at the company when you join."

Face-to-Face.   Negotiate in person, if possible. By making the effort to come to them, you show that you mean business and will sign during the visit if you can see your needs met.

Don't Make Demands.   Don't treat salary negotiations like a hardball session between a buyer and a seller of a car who will never see each other again. Consider it a problem-solving mission with the goal of making you a more loyal and satisfied employee. "Think of it as if you're going to see someone you really like," says Shell, "and you want to share some problems with them and enlist their help in solving the problems. For any problem there may be a hundred ways to solve it. That gets the other person engaged in helping you figure out the solution." Adds Taguchi: "View the negotiation as part of the relationship you are building with your potential new company."

A Good Opening Line.   "I'd really like to accept the offer and get started, but maybe you could help me with a few concerns so the job will fit better with my life."

And a Few Bad Ones.   "If the candidate just said, 'I'm not happy with my base salary' or 'I want to renegotiate that signing bonus,' that's an instant turn-off," says the recruiting director. "But if he or she said, 'By the way, I just wanted to know if there are any aspects to your package that are negotiable?' it speaks volumes. It's all in the approach."

Lay It All on the Table.   Avoid the "Oh, yeah, one more thing" style of negotiating. "If you start trickling things in, the employer will feel like they're getting nickel-and-dimed," says Shah. First they gave you extra on the bonus, and now you're asking for more vacation days; they gave you more vacation days, and now you're asking for more training. Present all of your concerns and desires up front and together. That way, you'll show that you've thought of everything.

Money Matters. When negotiating your salary, pick a goal slightly above the mean, as well as a bottom line—but keep these in perspective. If the company won't raise the base pay, for instance, what other perks might make the job worthwhile? A higher bonus? More vacation time? More training? Or maybe they can help pay off your student loans—and this sounds friendlier than asking for more salary.

Salary Deadlock Solution. Sometimes in large organizations, a starting pay grade will limit what your employer is allowed to negotiate, and any increase must wait until your first evaluation. So there's the fix—negotiate an early evaluation.

The Local Angle. If you don't need to relocate, you can use this fact to try to leverage a bigger bonus. Try: "I won't need the moving expenses, but it would be beneficial to channel such costs into a signing bonus." Include a good justification, such as putting a down payment on a home, which makes you look more attractive to the company.

Don't Ask for a Bandage in a Bar Fight. Be careful that your requests remain within the value system of the firm. "I had a guy who was interviewing for a high-risk type of financial job," says Shell. "Against my advice, he chose to negotiate a reduction in the amount of bonus compensation and an increase in base salary. Trying to negotiate your way out of risk at a risk-taking firm is going to send exactly the wrong signal. They withdrew the offer."

You Don't Say. Negotiations can bring up new and unexpected insights into a firm. "I had a situation where an MBA student was toying with an offer from a firm that was rumored to have been under an ethical black cloud a few years earlier," recalls a campus career counselor. "She asked for an opportunity to speak with a couple of former employees, and the head of the firm exploded, shouted at her on the phone, and withdrew the offer. We both saw that as a near miss. If she had gone to work there, who knows what would have been going on."

Pregnant Pauses. Silence is a great tactic in negotiations. It can make the other person nervous, and perhaps more willing to fill the void with talk of concessions. Just be still for ten seconds, and see what happens.

Signs of Trouble. If during your negotiations the other person answers his cell phone, checks his watch, or orders lunch on the speakerphone, you could be losing the battle.

Cheerlead. Show enthusiasm for the position and the company throughout the negotiation process. This can weaken your future employer's resolve and make her more willing to meet your demands. Also, in most instances, the person you are talking to will have to get a final approval, and you want her on your side. Stay just to this side of phoneydom, however. "We all know you love us," says the recruiter. "And we all know you've been coached."

In Writing.   If you come to an agreement, get the offer in writing. It should spell out the terms of your employment (salary, title, benefits, responsibilities, and so on). Look it over carefully to make sure everything is as agreed upon.

Sign Up Now.   There's no need to go back to your hotel and mull over the offer if you're getting what you need. By signing on the spot, you'll appear confident and motivated, and you'll set just the right tone for starting the job. "What people probably don't know is that how they behave in a process like this will always be extrapolated to how they are received at the company," says the recruiter. "Acting entitled can put a black mark on you before you come to the firm. It gets passed along to others before you even start." So behave.

But most of all, enjoy your new job.

INDEX

Index

Index